REBUILDING WITH HOPE

Who indeed despised the day of small beginnings?
Even they shall rejoice! (Zech. 4:10)

INTERNATIONAL THEOLOGICAL COMMENTARY

Fredrick Carlson Holmgren and George A. F. Knight

General Editors

Rebuilding with Hope

A Commentary on the Books of

Haggai and Zechariah

CARROLL STUHLMUELLER, C.P.

WM. B. EERDMANS PUBL. CO., GRAND RAPIDS

THE HANDSEL PRESS LTD. EDINBURGH

First published 1988 by Wm. B. Eerdmans Publishing Company,
255 Jefferson Ave. S.E., Grand Rapids, Michigan 49503
and
The Handsel Press Limited
33 Montgomery Street, Edinburgh EH7 5JX

Library of Congress Cataloging-in-Publication Data:

Stuhlmueller, Carroll.
Rebuilding with hope.

(International theological commentary)
Bibliography: p.
1. Bible.   O.T.   Haggai—Commentaries.
2. Bible.   O.T.   Zechariah—Commentaries.
I. Title.   II. Series.
BS1655.3.S78   1987   224'.9707   87-24546

Eerdmans ISBN 0-8028-2374-2
Handsel ISBN 0 905312 75 9

CONTENTS

ABBREVIATIONS

JB   Jerusalem Bible
JPSV   Jewish Publication Society Version
NAB   New American Bible
NEB   New English Bible
RSV   Revised Standard Version

EDITORS' PREFACE

The Old Testament alive in the Church: this is the goal of the *International Theological Commentary*. Arising out of changing, unsettled times, this Scripture speaks with an authentic voice to our own troubled world. It witnesses to God's ongoing purpose and to his caring presence in the universe without ignoring those experiences of life that cause one to question his existence and love. This commentary series is written by front-rank scholars who treasure the life of faith.

Addressed to ministers and Christian educators, the *International Theological Commentary* moves beyond the usual critical-historical approach to the Bible and offers a *theological* interpretation of the Hebrew text. Thus, engaging larger textual units of the biblical writings, the authors of these volumes assist the reader in the appreciation of the theology underlying the text as well as its place in the thought of the Hebrew Scriptures. But more, since the Bible is the book of the believing community, its text has acquired ever more meaning through an ongoing interpretation. This growth of interpretation may be found both within the Bible itself and in the continuing scholarship of the Church.

Contributors to the *International Theological Commentary* are Christians—persons who affirm the witness of the New Testament concerning Jesus Christ. For Christians, the Bible is *one* scripture containing the Old and New Testaments. For this reason, a commentary on the Old Testament may not ignore the second part of the canon, namely, the New Testament.

Since its beginning, the Church has recognized a special relationship between the two Testaments. But the precise character of this bond has been difficult to define. The diversity of views represented in these publications makes us aware that the Church is not of one mind in expressing the "how" of this relationship. The authors of this series share a developing consensus that any serious explanation of the Old Testament's relationship to the New will uphold the integrity of the Old Testament. Even though Christianity is rooted in the soil of the Hebrew Scriptures, the biblical interpreter must take care lest he "christianize" these Scriptures.

Authors writing in this commentary series will, no doubt, hold various views concerning *how* the Old Testament relates to the New. No attempt has been made to dictate one viewpoint in this matter. With the whole Church, we are convinced that the relationship between the two Testaments is real and substantial. But we recognize also the diversity of opinions among Christian scholars when they attempt to articulate fully the nature of this relationship.

In addition to the Christian Church, there exists another people for whom the Old Testament is important, namely, the Jewish community. Both Jews and Christians claim the Hebrew Bible as Scripture. Jews believe that the basic teachings of this Scripture point toward, and are developed by, the Talmud, which assumed its present form about 500 C.E. On the other hand, Christians hold that the Old Testament finds its fulfillment in the New Testament. The Hebrew Bible, therefore, belongs to both the Church and the Synagogue.

Recent studies have demonstrated how profoundly early Christianity reflects a Jewish character. This fact is not surprising because the Christian movement arose out of the context of first-century Judaism. Further, Jesus himself was Jewish, as were the first Christians. It is to be expected, therefore, that Jewish and Christian interpretations of the Hebrew Bible will reveal similarities *and* disparities. Such is the case. The authors of the *International Theological Commentary* will refer to the various Jewish traditions that they consider important for an appreciation of the Old Testament text. Such references will enrich our understanding of certain biblical passages and, as an extra gift, offer us insight into the relationship of Judaism to early Christianity.

An important second aspect of the present series is its *international* character. In the past, Western church leaders were considered to be *the* leaders of the Church—at least by those living in the West! The theology and biblical exegesis done by these scholars dominated the thinking of the Church. Most commentaries were produced in the Western world and reflected the lifestyle, needs, and thoughts of its civilization. But the Christian Church is a worldwide community. People who belong to the universal Church reflect differing thoughts, needs, and lifestyles.

Today the fastest growing churches in the world are to be found, not in the West, but in Africa, Indonesia, South America, Korea, Taiwan, and elsewhere. By the end of the century, Christians in these areas will outnumber those who live in the West. In our age, especially, a commentary on the Bible must transcend the parochialism of Western civilization and be sensitive to issues that are the special problems of persons who live outside the "Christian" West, issues such as race relations, personal survival and fulfillment, liberation, revolution, famine, tyranny, disease, war, the poor, religion and state. Inspired by God, the authors of the Old Testament knew what life is like on the edge of existence. They addressed themselves to everyday people who often faced more than everyday problems. Refusing to limit God to the "spiritual," they portrayed him as one who heard and knew the cries of people in pain (see Exod. 3:7-8). The contributors to the *International Theological Commentary* are persons who prize the writings of these biblical authors as a word of life to our world today. They read the Hebrew Scriptures in the contexts of ancient Israel and our modern day.

The scholars selected as contributors underscore the international aspect of the Commentary. Representing very different geographical, ideological, and ecclesiastical backgrounds, they come from over seventeen countries. Besides scholars from such traditional countries as England, Scotland, France, Italy, Switzerland, Canada, New Zealand, Australia, South Africa, and the United States, contributors from the following places are included: Israel, Indonesia, India, Thailand, Singapore, Taiwan, and countries of Eastern Europe. Such diversity makes for richness of thought. Christian scholars living in Buddhist, Muslim, or Socialist lands may be able to offer the World Church insights into the biblical message—insights to which the scholarship of the West could be blind.

The proclamation of the biblical message is the focal concern of the *International Theological Commentary*. Generally speaking, the authors of these commentaries value the historical-critical studies of past scholars, but they are convinced that these studies by themselves are not enough. The Bible is more than an object of critical study; it is the revelation of God. In the written Word, God has disclosed himself and his will to humankind. Our authors see themselves as servants of the Word which, when rightly received, brings *shalom* to both the individual and the community.

—George A. F. Knight
—Fredrick Carlson Holmgren

With Appreciation
to
My Brothers in the Congregation of the Passion
at
The Catholic Theological Union in Chicago

A Commentary on the Book of
Haggai

CONTENTS

INTRODUCTION

FROM PHOPHECY TO THE PROPHETS
HAGGAI AND ZECHARIAH

As far back as 1916 Bernhard Duhm declared very simply that prophecy has its history. In its nature and manifestation it has passed through many forms. In one of his early books, *The Conscience of Israel* (7), Bruce Vawter wrote, "If we are to understand correctly the prophets and what they said, . . . there is no substitute for seeing them against the backdrop of the history in which they lived."

As we turn to the prophets Haggai and Zechariah, we are crossing a "continental divide" in the history of prophecy. Yet even if history includes dramatic changes, continuity is also an essential ingredient. No matter how different be the culture and sociological setting of any new generation, even if the children cross oceans in pursuit of the new world, still they carry the genes of their ancestors. They will adapt and evolve, but they remain essentially the children of their forebears. Haggai and Zechariah, no matter how dramatic be the change in prophecy with their preaching and writing, bear the marks of tradition. They bring prophecy back to its starting point in sanctuary worship (cf. 1 Sam. 9).

Earlier prophetic bands in the books of Samuel and Kings addressed kings and were closely associated with worship and politics; classical prophecy, which begins with Amos and Hosea and continues with Isaiah and Jeremiah, enlarged its audience to include *all* the people of Israel. Classical prophecy, moreover, strongly and at times bitterly criticized kings, priests, and even fellow prophets who functioned in the sanctuaries. Amos, the first of the classical prophets, refused even to be called either a prophet or a member of any prophetic band (Amos 7:14). Micah lashes out at sanctuary personnel:

> Its heads give judgment for a bribe,
> its priests teach for hire,

> its prophets divine for money;
> yet they lean upon the LORD and say,
> > "Is not the LORD in the midst of us?
> > No evil shall come upon us."
> Therefore, because of you
> > Zion shall be plowed as a field;
> Jerusalem shall become a heap of ruins,
> > and the mountain of the house a wooded height.
> > > > > (Mic. 3:11-12)

The demise of sanctuary worship, threatened by Micah, actually happened in 587 B.C. Some sixty years later, however, with a memory of the Exile behind the people, Haggai and Zechariah led prophecy back in many ways to defend sanctuary worship and to affirm the role of the Davidic royalty and of the temple priesthood. From a closer scrutiny of prophecy in its various historical moments, we will realize that changes were necessary in order to remain true to the initial inspiration of Israel's religion from the days of Moses.

Origins and Development of Prophecy

The origins of prophecy rest firmly on two or three statements within the Ten Commandments:

> I am the LORD your God, who brought you out of the land of Egypt, out of the house of bondage. You shall have no other gods before me. . . . You shall remember that you were a servant in the land of Egypt, and the LORD your God brought you out thence with a mighty hand and an outstretched arm. (Deut. 5:6-7, 15)

Prophecy, more than any other institution in Israel, defended the rights of slaves and underprivileged people to compassion and dignity, as well as the rights of Yahweh for exclusive worship and love. Prophecy also proclaimed that Yahweh will stop at nothing to achieve and sustain these divine goals for the chosen people.

Another passage of Deuteronomy, recording this faith-filled, visionary prayer of Moses, offers another clue to the essential characteristics of prophecy:

> O Lord GOD, thou hast only begun to show thy servant thy greatness and thy mighty hand; for what god is there in heaven or on earth who can do such works and mighty acts as thine? (Deut. 3:24)

While looking closely to earthly matters and the basic rights of people, as in Deut. 5:16-21, a prophet also rightly earned the title of seer, according to Deut. 3:24, peering into the heavens and proclaiming the distant future. Each prophet in his or her own way was such a seer; Haggai and Zechariah will give the role of seer or visionary ever more importance.

While conscious of the heavens, prophets felt the warm earth between their toes and heard the cry of the poor. From the time of Moses and his successor Joshua, we find several almost parenthetical remarks about Israel that are like the seeds from which later prophecy's concern for the poor will develop:

"A mixed multitude also went up with them" (Exod. 12:38). "Now the rabble that was among them had a strong craving" (Num. 11:4).

"Then Joshua built an altar in Mount Ebal to the LORD, the God of Israel. . . . And all Israel, sojourner as well as home-born, with their elders and officers and their judges, stood on opposite sides of the ark" (Josh. 8:30, 33).

Putting these passages together we find that Israel was never a pure-blooded people that stemmed from a single ancestry or from an isolated geographical location, nor did Israel emerge from any single social class or cultural milieu. As the texts in Exodus and Numbers put it, Israel was a "mixed-up" "rabble." Prophecy never forgot the lowly, untractable origins of Israel. It highlighted still other ingredients from early history that made Israel to be Israel: chosen not by reason of any human prerogatives but by the Lord's free and compassionate choice of the oppressed (cf. Deut. 7:6-11); endowed like Moses with charismatic gifts that reached into the secret potential of the people. Prophecy evolved through its recognition and defense of the rights of the poor; Haggai and Zechariah represent an important stage in that evolution.

Prophecy was of critical importance in the life of Israel, but, surprisingly to us, it was not the primary source of Israel's survival. Prophecy was always interacting with Israel's other, more permanent and more central institutions, its civil and religious authorities in palace and temple. Prophecy at times supported them, at times it challenged and purified them. Prophecy even announced their destruction that they may emerge with new strength. Israel would never have survived without its tradition of laws and customs, without its meeting place for worship and remembrance, without its organizational leaders in priests and levites, kings and elders, plus the earlier bands of prophets clustering around sanctuary and palace (cf. Deut. 17–18). It was this organizational leadership that actually preserved the great acts and preaching of the prophets.

Throughout its history prophecy lived at the eye of the hurricane, or shall we say in the heart of a transcendent, jealous yet immanent and compassionate God. As the environment changed, so did the attitude of prophets. They were found, functioning within the sanctuary (1 Sam. 9:11-26) and condemning the sanctuary (Mic. 3:12; Jer. 26:1-19), announcing Israel's destruction by gentile nations (Isa. 10:5-6) and seeing a vision of the Gentiles coming peacefully to the temple (Isa. 2:2-5), anointing kings (1 Sam. 10:1) and condemning kings for oppressing their own poor (Jer. 22:10-30). While these various moments came separately in the preexilic history of Israel, they were compressed within the short span of the prophets Haggai and Zechariah.

How the transition was made from the Exile to the beginning of the postexilic age when Haggai and Zechariah appeared needs to be explored more carefully. The generations closest to a child will have the strongest influence. As mentioned already, prophecy despite its complexity remained faithful to the basic traditions.

From Exile to Homeland

Prophecy is complex because it is intertwined with the complex history of Israel. The Babylonian conquerors of Jerusalem in 587 B.C. (2 Kgs. 25), like the Assyrian conquerors of Samaria in 721 (2 Kgs. 17), deported religious and civil leaders, artisans, builders and other tradespeople; the Assyrians, but not the Babylonians, brought other captive peoples into the land of Israel. Each left behind a few Israelites, "the poorest of the land to be vinedressers and plowmen" (2 Kgs. 24:14; 25:12).

Life was extremely difficult after 587. The local inhabitants, without walled cities and therefore almost defenseless, faced invasion from the Edomites to the south; the pain and rage of people, kicked and abused in their misery, still echoes in prophecy (cf. Obad. 12-14; Isa. 63:1-6). The people who remained in the land suffered from serious dissent among themselves (Jer. 40–44). Some of them continued the practice of going to the ruined temple to present "cereal offerings and incense" (Jer. 41:5). We owe the book of Lamentations, as S. Paul Re'emi wrote in another volume of this series (*God's People in Crisis,* 80-81), to this group of devout Israelites in the devastated homeland.

As mentioned already, the Assyrians "brought people from Babylon, Cuthah, Avva, Hamath and Sepharvaim, and placed them in the cities of Samaria" (2 Kgs. 17:24). Later in the same chapter we read that "the king of Assyria commanded, 'Send there one of the priests whom you carried away thence; and let him go and dwell there, and teach them the law of the god of the land.' [He] taught them how they should fear the Lord" (vv. 27-28).

These people then, both in Samaria and Judah, at times divided and misled, subject to invasion and many natural hardships, held on for dear life. Many of them, like the author(s) of Lamentations, mourned the loss of the temple and prayed for the reconstruction of Israel. Suffering as they did for their faith and remaining faithful in the land of the ancestors, they felt that they were the true remnant, the core of the future Israel. Haggai did not agree with their claims (cf. Hag. 2:10-14). See G. A. F. Knight, *The New Israel,* xii-xiii.

The complexities of history continued among the other group of Israelites, those in exile. Religious and civil leaders among them preserved and at times adapted the ancient customs and statements of faith. A new edition of what scholars call the Priestly tradition and the Deuteronomic tradition of Mosaic times was prepared. While the Priestly tradition generally represented Mosaic customs, laws and stories as taught and applied at Jerusalem, the Deuteronomic tradition did the same for those handed down in the northern sanctuaries and capital.

The southern traditions at Jerusalem tended to be more stern, more centralized, more cultic; the northern traditions breathed more compassion, more stress upon the home as the place of instruction and worship, with a wider outreach in religious leadership. One can compare the two editions of the Decalogue about sabbath observance (Exod. 20:8-11; Deut. 5:12-15). Or consider the recognition of leadership in many parts of the country in Deut. 18 as compared with the more restricted focusing upon Aaron and the more careful regulations for other Levites in Num. 3; 16-17. While the northern traditions were closer to the Mosaic covenant and the wilderness experience in Sinai, the southern traditions were more solidly based on the covenant with David and on the ritual of the Jerusalem temple.

Other serious differences, eventually to affect the prophecies of Haggai and Zechariah, appear during the Exile, especially in the two great prophetic figures, Second Isaiah and Ezekiel. Second Isaiah, whose preaching is recorded in Isa. 40–55, voiced northern sympathies and theology; Ezekiel was undoubtedly the spokesperson for the southern traditions, as these survived among the exiles (not among the people left behind in the devastated land around Jerusalem). Ezekiel sees the glory of the Lord leave the temple and come to rest to the east on the Mount of Olives (Ezek. 11:22-23); the Lord has abandoned the inhabitants left behind in Jerusalem. Second Isaiah sings of the glory of the Lord accompanying the people through foreign territory on the way back to their own land (Isa. 40:3-5). While Second Isaiah mentions the Jerusalem temple only once, and that in a disputed half-verse (Isa. 44:28b), Ezekiel centers the final part of his prophecy around the Jerusalem temple from which flows life-giving water (cf. Ezek. 40–48, esp. 47:1-12). In still another contrast Second Isaiah speaks more openly of servant messengers and extends leadership more generously to all the people (cf. Isa. 52:1-12); Ezekiel for his part concentrates on the exclusive privileges of the Zadokite priests (who were Levites with a capital *L*) and demotes the other Levites (Ezek. 40:46; 44:10-31). Second Isaiah seems to blur the image of Davidic royalty by returning its privileges to the people (Isa. 55:3-5, where the "you" is plural in Hebrew and refers to all Israel); Ezekiel, on the contrary, recognizes, though with diminution, the privileges of the Davidic kings (Ezek. 46:2, 10).

Haggai and Zechariah, we shall see, belong to the southern traditions and trace their prophetic pedigree to Ezekiel.

Upon the return from exile, the major question can be phrased in this way: *who is the true remnant?* Is it those who remained in the land and were not a part of the theological and liturgical developments of the Exile? If so, were the Samaritans to be included? Or is it the party that rallied around Second Isaiah? Or is the remnant the exclusive prerogative of those returnees whose spirit is supremely in line with the revised Priestly tradition of the Torah and the prophetic preaching of Ezekiel? Haggai, whose prophecy seems colorless and insignificant at first reading, became God's agent responsible for unequivocally answering these questions.

Theological Currents in the Early Postexilic Age

The reestablishment of Israel in its homeland will quite naturally resemble the first establishment under Joshua. The difficulties are enormous and people are called to heroic response. The need for structure and leadership will be recognized. Prophets, now as in the past, supported the experiment of new leadership and joined the ranks of civil and religious leaders. Elders, for instance in the days of Moses, were endowed with prophetic charism (Num. 11:16-17, 24-30), and the prophet Samuel and the bands of ecstatic prophets were active in the choice of the first kings (1 Sam. 8–10, 16).

Organizational types of leadership and their affirmation by prophetic blessing will become a prominent feature in Haggai and Zechariah. Classical prophecy that challenged and condemned kings and priests in the preexilic period now reverts back to the form of the early prophetic bands. Yet the touch of classical prophecy remains with Haggai and Zechariah in that a sense of future divine intervention is perceived:

> Once again, in a little while, I will shake the heavens and the earth and the sea and the dry land; and I will shake all nations, so that the treasures of all nations shall come in, and I will fill this house with splendor, says the Lord of hosts. . . . The latter splendor of this house shall be greater than the former, says the Lord of hosts; and in this place I will give prosperity, says the Lord of hosts (Hag. 2:6-9).

The sense of God's future intervention takes a dramatic turn in the night visions of Zechariah (cf. Zech. 1:8). This visionary style will become still more fearful and its effects all the more unearthly in the second part of Zechariah (chs. 9-14).

Another, somewhat different postexilic temple tradition occurs in the two books of Chronicles. Here the centering upon the Jerusalem sanctuary is still more exalted, as though one does not have to wait for the shaking of the heavens and the shaking of the earth announced by Haggai. In these books prophecy is identified with temple singers:

> David and the chiefs of the service also set apart for the service certain of the sons of Asaph, and of Heman, and of Jeduthun, *who should prophesy with lyres, with harps, and with cymbals* (1 Chr. 25:1).

The splendor of temple ritual with its strong symbolism and elaborate ceremonies anticipates the future. Eschatology, Israel's hopes for the final day, is seen to be already present in the moment of worship.

As mentioned already with regard to Zech. 9–14, prophecy is affirming ever more emphatically Yahweh's momentous intervention, sometime in the future. This attitude will become paramount in what is called apocalyptic literature, such as Dan. 7–12; but earlier stages are detected in some of the first literature of the postexilic age: in Haggai, Zechariah, Joel, Mal. 3, and Isa. 24–27. In this literature we see the transition from eschatology (focusing on the "end time," as the word means) to apocalypticism (focusing on what lies beyond the end with the breakup of earthly structures and the vision of the unearthly—the word means "drawing aside the veil").

Finally, we note the wisdom movement that offers little or no attention to such items as the temple and its ritual, salvation history and its account of Yahweh's wondrous intervention, prophetic challenge and eschatological preoccupation. Wisdom in the book of Proverbs focuses upon the here and now and what is humanly possible with moderation. This tradition continues into the literature of Job, Song of Songs, and Ecclesiastes. While Job will manifest considerable interaction with various prophetic traditions, still the dominant attitude is that inherited from the wisdom tradition.

Little doubt remains among scholars where Haggai and Zechariah were most congenially at home among these various theological currents: strong temple orientation; seconding the authority of the Zadokite priesthood; walking according to the momentum and stride of the prophet Ezekiel; at first confident in the Davidic dynasty; leaning towards the eschatological; hinting at the apocalyptic; in no way concerned with sapiential piety. It is no small tribute to Haggai that his preaching set the stage for what was to become the dominant spirituality of postexilic Israel. The book is small, the second smallest in the Hebrew Scriptures, but its impact is mighty.

Postexilic Prophetical Literature

For the most part the age of creative or innovative prophetical preaching is over. In accord with a pattern already discernible in the preaching of Jeremiah (Jer. 26:18; 31:29; cf. Ezek. 18:2), prophecy is quoting prophecy. The Bible is no longer a tradition creatively open to new forms and ideas, but is beginning to resemble Christian piety in that the Bible is quoting the Bible! At the very least we see increasingly more evidence of inspired redactors, collecting and organizing earlier inspired preaching and writing.

Relying upon the studies of David L. Petersen, *Late Israelite Prophecy* (ch. 2), we recognize the following characteristics of postexilic prophetical literature: 1) the tendency to gather earlier works and to edit them with an eye to new circumstances; 2) the attachment of these new collections to the tradition from which they stem, e.g., Isa. 40–55 and 56–66 together with Isa. 13–23 and 24–27 are added to the book of Isaiah; 3) the care to balance prophetic threats with promise and hope, particularly for temple ceremony (see the sequence of hope for Jerusalem in Mic. 4 after the dreadful threat against the temple at the end of ch. 3); 4) the addition of liturgical formulae (i.e., the hymnic fragments added in Amos 4:13; 5:8; 9:5-6). Prophecy was depending upon the authority of the earlier prophetic masters as well as upon acceptance in temple ritual, if it was to be canonized in this later age.

THE PROPHET HAGGAI WITHIN HIS TIMES

The Prophet

The features on Haggai's face seem to blur before us. It is difficult to catch the lines of family background, age, character, and other personal details. We depend almost solely upon the book by his name, which after the prophecy of Obadiah is the shortest in the Hebrew Scriptures. Haggai, moreover, so identifies himself with rebuilding the temple and reestablishing Davidic authority that his own personality is hidden from the reader. People in exalted places can easily be absorbed within their office; temple ceremony and its elaborate symbolism can wrap Levite or priest beneath many layers of sacred vestments and behind clouds of incense. Unlike preexilic prophets whose sole authority was the conviction of their conscience, Haggai was not forced to reveal too many of the tensions of his private person. In this respect he differs especially from such prophets as Hosea and Jeremiah.

Haggai is mentioned twice in the book of Ezra along with with his contemporary, Zechariah, each time urging the people to proceed with rebuilding the temple of the Lord in Jerusalem (Ezra 5:1; 6:14). Yet, the separate books of Haggai and Zechariah never link the two men together. We are left, therefore, with some curious questions: was there a personality clash, for in a small place like Jerusalem surely the two prophets had to know one another? Was there jealousy between them? The Bible, however, does not cater to our curiosity nor to our proneness to quick judgments! As we shall see, Zechariah preached for a longer period of time and to that extent eclipsed Haggai.

Haggai becomes a still more lonely figure when we remember that his name, in the form we have it, never occurs again in the Hebrew Scriptures. Similar forms are found, such as Haggi in Gen. 46:16, or Haggiah in 1 Chr. 6:30, and Haggith in 2 Sam. 3:4. All are variations upon the Hebrew word for feast or religious festival

11

(hag). This word, accordingly, may include dancing or pilgrimage (1 Kgs. 8:65; 12:32-33; Ps. 118:27; Neh. 8:18). For these reasons some suggest that Haggai's name may imply that he was born on a major feast day, perhaps the Feast of Tabernacles; the latter is sometimes simply called "the feast" (Neh. 8:14, 18; Ps. 81:3). If the idea of religious festivals helps to break the loneliness around Haggai, he slips back into obscurity from the fact that his father's name is not mentioned, something unusual for a people who had no family name but were identified through father and mother.

Can we go a step forward and from his name, *Haggai* or *Festival,* infer that he was a priest? About the only other evidence for this claim is his direction in Hag. 2:11: "Ask the priests to decide this question." Such advice, however, can just as easily be interpreted to mean that he was not among the priests to whom he was sending the people. No Jewish tradition, moreover, links Haggai with the tribe of Levi or the priestly family of Zadok.

Was Haggai an older man? In fact, can we say that as a young boy he was among those who were never deported but left behind in the land in 587 B.C., some sixty-seven years before he began to prophesy? The returnees from exile, however, different from Haggai, usually show up with a careful genealogy, as we find in the early chapters of the book of Ezra. Zechariah at least is favored with his father's name! Haggai's close association with the disciples and traditions of Ezekiel argues against his belonging to the local people of the land; the Ezekiel party eventually rejected all contact with these people (cf. Ezra 9–10). The most we can say is that Haggai knew well the conditions of the land around 520 and spoke with conviction about it.

The Times

If Haggai spoke of the shaking of the heavens and of the earth (Hag. 2:6), such, indeed, was the situation in his lifetime. The Persian Empire was convulsing with intrigue, revolt, and civil war. Cambyses (530-522 B.C.), son and successor of the founder of the empire and of the Achaemenian Dynasty, Cyrus the Great, died in Palestine on his return from an Egyptian campaign. Another son of Cyrus, Bardiya by name, was captured and killed by a member of the Achaemenian family named Darius. For two years, 522-520, Darius faced revolts against his authority. Later, while commemorating his victories on the famous Behistun Inscription, Darius offered another explanation, that the man he killed was a royal pretender who resembled Bardiya. See Joseph Blenkinsopp, *A History of Prophecy in Israel,* 231.

After the shaking of the heavens and the earth ceased with the return of peace, Darius continued the benevolent policies of Cyrus. He encouraged local rule and codification of local laws and customs, the rebuilding of sanctuaries and their use for administrative purposes.

Haggai's prophecy echoes these two sides of Darius' reign: *the upheavals* that for Haggai triggered new hopes for the great transformation of Judah; *the political peace* that permitted the Jews to reconstruct the temple and reconstitute clear lines of religious and secular authority.

The Place

Haggai prophesied at Jerusalem, a city that lay in ruins, without the protection of walls, and set amidst a countryside that was wasted by drought (Hag. 1:9-11). The city, formerly with more than 100,000 inhabitants, now numbered no more than 30,000, if that many.

Politically the place was called Yehud, an Aramaic variation on Judah, the name of the southern kingdom before the Exile. While some historians claim that Yehud was administered through a governor at Samaria, Geo Widengren offers good reasons that Persia accepted the previous arrangements set up by the Assyrians and Babylonians. The Assyrians, conquering Samaria in 721 B.C., made it a separate province; the Babylonians, destroying much of Judah in 587, left it alone and desolate, controlled directly from Babylon. Only later in 482 was the whole territory of Samaria and Judah reorganized and absorbed within the larger satrap called "Beyond the River [Euphrates]." See Geo Widengren, "The Persian Period," *Israelite and Judaean History,* ed. John H. Hayes and J. Maxwell Miller, 509-511.

The Date of Haggai

The editor dates each of Haggai's sermons—although, as we shall see, there is some confusion in the arrangement and number of them. The first is placed "in the second year of Darius the king, in the sixth month, on the first day of the month" (Hag. 1:1), which would be 29 August 520 B.C. (cf. Jack Finegan, *Handbook of Biblical Chronology,* 212-13). The final sermon "on the twenty-fourth day of the [ninth] month" (2:20; cf. v. 10) took place on 18 December 520. This method of recording year and day in Haggai is reminiscent of Ezekiel (e.g., Ezek. 1:1; 8:1; 20:1). After this brief appearance within less than four months, Haggai disappeared. His work was done: people had earnestly set to work on rebuilding the temple; Zerubbabel was recognized as governor of Yehud and heir of the Davidic promises.

STRUCTURE AND FORM
OF THE PROPHECY OF HAGGAI

Stages of Formation

Like previous classical prophets, Haggai's book began as an *oral* message that was only later written down and edited. It is possible—but again the fact is wrapped in obscurity—that Haggai preached more often than what is recorded, perhaps regularly within the religious services at Jerusalem.

The editor's hand is seen quite often for a book as small as Haggai's. To this person is attributed the dating, introductory formulas, and reports on the effect of the preaching; all of these references to Haggai are in the third person. Altogether these editorial segments are found in:

1:1, 3, 12, 13a, 14, 15
2:1, 2?, 10, 13a, 14a, 20.

Following the lead of Rex A. Mason ("The Purpose of the Editorial Framework of the Book of Haggai," *VT* 27 [1977]: 415-421), we compare these editorial remarks with other books of the Bible. We thus find important links with the prophet Ezekiel as well as with the traditions associated with Deuteronomy, the Priestly tradition and Chronicles.

The phrase, "the word of the Lord came by [literally, by the hand of] Haggai the prophet" (Hag. 1:1, 3; 2:1, with an alternate form in 2:10, 20) is found in similar form four times in the work of the Chronicler and thirteen times in the Priestly tradition of the Pentateuch. In many of these cases the phrase refers to Moses as lawgiver and to temple concerns (e.g., 2 Chr. 29:25; Exod. 39:29; Lev. 10:11; 26:46).

Another phrase, used by Haggai of Joshua and Zerubbabel, "take courage" (Hag. 2:4) occurs in the Deuteronomistic writings by way of encouragement to the people (Deut. 31:6, 7, 23) and to Moses' successor, Joshua (Josh. 1:6, 7, 9) and by Joshua to the people (Josh. 10:25). Or again, a word that Haggai introduces in Hag. 1:14, "to work" on the house of the Lord, is found in the Priestly tradition of Exod. 35:29; 36:2 of work on the tabernacle.

The editor, accordingly, was associating the new temple of the early postexilic period with the tabernacle in the days of Moses and with the temple of Solomon. The great founders of Israel were seen to be living again in the new leadership of Haggai's time. Haggai's close ties with Ezekiel, the Jerusalem temple, and priesthood were reaffirmed by the editor.

After blending a traditional theology of temple and settlement of the land into the preaching of Haggai, the editor selected four or five sermons (originally were there more?) and arranged them in the form of a book. The larger structural pattern within the book is presented as follows by Théophane Chary (*Aggée—Zacharie Malachie*, 12):

Criticism of people	Hag. 1:1-5	2:10-14
Their miserable condition	1:6-11	2:15-17
Return to grace	1:12-14	2:18-19
"Messianic" oracle	2:2-9	2:20-23

Outline of the Book

1:1-14	First intervention of Haggai, first day, sixth month
1:15a + 2:15-19	Oracle on twenty-fourth day, sixth month
1:15b + 2:1-9	Oracle on twenty-first day, seventh month
2:10-14	Consultation of Haggai and the priests, twenty-fourth day, ninth month
2:20-23	Oracle on twenty-fourth day, ninth month

Style

Haggai spoke in a way that mirrored his times. Zechariah the prophet characterized this age as "the day of small things" and asked that it not be despised (Zech. 4:10). The city lay in ruins, drought had left the countryside brown and gasping for life. The melodious poetry of Second and Third Isaiah (Isa. 40–55; 56–66) and the lofty visions of First Isaiah (2:2-5; ch. 6), and even the intense pleading of Jeremiah would have collapsed ridiculously in this setting. Alone among the prophets, Haggai spoke in prose, with only an occasional rhythm in the messianic visions. This meagre and starved style, as George Adam Smith described it long ago (*The Book of the Twelve Prophets* 2:237), was in harmony with the occasion. We judge the achievement of Haggai, not by the beauty of his style but by the effectiveness of his preaching. Perhaps alone among the prophets he saw the fruits of his faithful preaching.

THE MESSAGE OF HAGGAI

Two Centers

Haggai's focus was exceptionally clear. All of his energies were directed towards two goals: the rebuilding of the temple and the restoration of the Davidic rule.

He refers in many striking ways to the temple: as "the house (Hebrew *bet*) of the LORD" (Hag. 1:2), as the house in which God takes pleasure (1:8), as "my house" (1:9), as "palace (*hekal*; RSV "temple") of the LORD" (2:15). The rebuilding of the temple celebrated Israel's survival of the ordeal of the Exile and its restoration to new life. The new temple linked Haggai's day with the courageous and creative periods of Moses and Joshua, David and Solomon. It announced a determination to renew the remembrance of Israel's great moments of salvation under these charismatic leaders, true servants of the Lord.

Haggai realized that God's great redemptive acts for the chosen people Israel could have been forgotten had they not been celebrated with each new generation at temple liturgy. If these events were no different than what was happening to many other migrating nations (cf. Amos 9:7), the difference lies in Israel's faith to recognize that *Yahweh was acting* in these events and through these leaders in Israel's behalf. Liturgy confessed and celebrated this faith. In a true sense liturgy turned small events, not recorded in world annals of ancient times, into significant events in world history even today.

In prodding the people to rebuild the temple, Haggai made sure that the postexilic restoration would not consist exclusively in the political acts of the Persians nor in the revival of Israel's economy. The prophet perceived the strong presence of Yahweh within the politics and economics of his age. Yahweh was achieving what seemed humanly impossible: a future glory that would surpass the glory of Solomon's temple. To this extent Haggai's vision extended beyond that of the Chronicler who concentrated almost solely upon the Second Temple of the postexilic age (cf. 2 Chr. 36:22-23).

The restoration of the Davidic dynasty was to be the last chance at government by this family. Haggai would not let Israel neutralize the everlasting promises to David, as Second Isaiah was willing to do (Isa. 55:3). Haggai was truly a man of tradition; changes would be accepted, but only as God brought them about. Haggai would be more attentive to governor Zerubbabel than the prophet Zechariah, whose book at least allowed this Davidic heir to pass from the scene (cf. Zech. 6:9-14). As mentioned already, Haggai was accepting the practice of the Persians in permitting local rule according to the people's traditions.

Haggai's opposition to local people whose parents or ancestors had not been deported by the Assyrians and Babylonians (cf. Hag. 2:10-14) brought Israel a step forward in achieving its racial purity and separate identity as Yahweh's chosen people.

Religious Adaptation of Tradition

We have noted the main theological currents within the work of Haggai and his editor, namely: (1) Ezekiel and the Priestly tradition of the Pentateuch, major representatives of the southern Jerusalem theology; (2) a blend of the Deuteronomic tradition with that of the Chronicler, so that Yahweh was seen to give strength for the work of rebuilding the temple; (3) a loyalty to the Davidic dynasty but with particular emphasis placed upon the temple as central to Israel's survival, a movement away from a political state to one that is ever more theocratic.

Differing from the Chronicler, Haggai did not stress the brilliance of temple liturgy, but rather directed hopes toward the eschatological future after the final shaking of the heavens and of the earth. Yahweh, rather than any political power in the Davidic dynasty, will accomplish this shaking. Prophecy, therefore, takes a firm step forward, away from its preexilic concern with social reform for the poor and religious purification of the cult—away from the present moment to what the future holds in store. Other prophets of the early postexilic period, however, like Zechariah 1–8 and Third Isaiah tilt the scales again more firmly towards concern for poor and neglected people.

Haggai did not suggest any timetable for this future fulfillment; that crucial aspect lay in Yahweh's control (cf. Brevard S. Childs, *Introduction to the Old Testament as Scripture*, 471). Yet neither was it so far away as to be beyond human hope. Haggai speaks of "a little while" (Hag. 2:6), and he also picks up a Deuteronomic phrase, "on that day" (v. 23).

BRING WOOD AND
BUILD THE HOUSE
Haggai 1:1-14

CLEARLY ADDRESSING THE SITUATION

To appreciate the theological message of Haggai, it is necessary to recognize how this prophet looked directly into his own age and addressed the situation in clear, blunt, and unadorned language. Even though Hag. 1:1-14 turns out rather complex with many editorial additions (i.e., the introductory phrases at vv. 3a, 5a, 7a, 13a), nonetheless, Haggai's statement is unmistakable. Haggai adopted a standard but forceful prophetical style. There are three oracles of Yahweh either in the form of a disputation with the people, similar to those in Amos (Amos 8:5-6) and Second Isaiah (Isa. 45:9-13), or else in the more elaborate form of a lawcourt scene (Isa. 1:2-3, 10-17). Although Haggai's prophecy is stylistically simple, he makes good use of a key Hebrew word to hold things together and to heighten the momentum of the oral delivery: *hareb* in Hag. 1:4, 9 speaks of "ruins"; *horeb* in 1:11 refers to the "drought"; *harabah* in 2:6 means "dry land." For the people to have left the temple *in ruins* brought on the punishment of the *drought*, but the rebuilding of the temple will issue in a "shaking" or renewal of "the heavens and the earth and the sea and *the dry land*."

As mentioned already in the introduction, Haggai's preaching reflects the revolts in the first years of the reign of Darius I, son of Hystaspes (522-486 B.C.). Eventually this monarch extended the Persian Empire to its farthest limits: in the southwest to Lybia, in the northwest to Thrace and the Danube River, and in the east as far as India. This penetration into Greece led to Darius' defeat at the famous battle of Marathon (490). Yet Haggai will focus instead upon a single event at Jerusalem, the rebuilding of the temple. Here is one instance among many in the Bible where a very selective approach is taken to history. Historical details are not chosen for their importance on the world scene but for their theological impact upon the chosen people Israel.

For the rebuilding of the temple Haggai needed the cooperation of Zerubbabel, the Jewish governor. Zerubbabel (the Hebrew word means "seed of Babylon") is not to be identified with Shesh-bazzar who initially began the rebuilding of the temple, as we are told within the Aramaic annals in Ezra 5:14-16. This individual disappeared from history and his work came to nothing. Shesh-bazzar was succeeded by his nephew, Zerubbabel, born to the former king Jehoiachin's eldest son, Shealtiel. (According to 1 Chr. 3:19 he was the son of Pedaiah, who may have been the natural father while his legal father, through the levirate marriage, was Shealtiel. For levirate marriage, see Deut. 25:5-10.)

Still another person will sooner or later eclipse Zerubbabel, especially in the preaching of Zechariah. He too is mentioned in the superscription to Haggai's prophecy. He is Joshua the high priest (this is the first time the title is used in Jewish history), the grandson of Seraiah, killed by the Babylonians at the destruction of Jerusalem, and the son of Jehozadak who was taken into exile (cf. 1 Chr. 6:14-15; 2 Kgs. 25:8-11).

Haggai begins prophesying on the "first day of the sixth month." This day corresponds to August 29, 520. During the Exile the Jewish people adopted the Assyrian-Babylonian method of calculating the year from spring to spring. Accordingly, the ceremony of New Year's Day, as described in Lev. 23:24-25 and Num. 29:1-6, is placed at the beginning of the "seventh month," a curious blend of the old and new calendars.

To achieve the purpose of his preaching Haggai points to the paneled houses (Hag. 1:4) of the governor and high priest, luxurious when compared with the people's homes. The comparison with the temple was all the more startling. Is this style of living proper, he asks, "while this house [of the Lord, and now he points in another direction] lies in ruins"? There may have been a touch of angry sarcasm in his voice, for neither he nor the rest of the people could afford such extravagance. Or else Haggai speaks with irony that the governor and high priest pretend to mimic the elaborate building plans of King Solomon (1 Kgs. 6:9; 7:3, 7) or worse still that they appear like the wily and wicked Jehoiakim, who pretended to be a great king by building "a great house with spacious upper rooms, . . . [paneled] with cedar" (Jer. 22:14). Haggai spoke with directness and conviction, in a prosaic style completely in accord with this "day of small things" (Zech. 4:10). Haggai, therefore, was very effective, first because he focused the long history of Israel and its religious traditions immediately upon the present moment, and second because of his common sense to implement ideas with an achievable plan of work.

TEMPLE, COVENANT, AND THE EXTERNAL FORMS OF RELIGION

Haggai could never be satisfied with a private religion of the heart or home. To achieve his goal, he turned to the Mosaic covenant and its traditions of blessings or curses depending upon Israel's obedience or disobedience. Like everything else, Haggai's contact with the covenant is through the temple. Therefore, he concluded, the temple must be rebuilt. In Hag. 1:6, 9-11 his lines remind us particularly of the curses and blessings that enter the covenant formula and correspond to Israel's compliance or not with its agreement with the Lord. These blessings and curses reach into the land and the climate as well as into Israel's interaction with neighboring nations (see Deut. 28). If Israel should be disobedient to the Lord, drought will strike the land (Deut 28:23-24) and the harvest will be insufficient (Deut 28:15-19, 38-40). Food and clothing will be sufficient if Israel is faithful (Deut 10:18). Haggai's statements also reflect a strong prophetical stance, that Yahweh will direct the foreign nations to converge upon Israel from all directions to punish the people if the Israelites "do not return to me," according to the formula of Amos (Amos 4:6-12).

Religion, or better the God of the covenant, is at the heart of Israel's existence. If Israel is not obedient to the Lord nothing will succeed, whether it be politics or farming, family health or national dignity. Even the climate and other natural phenomena depend upon Israel's relationship with the Lord. From the books of Deuteronomy and of Haggai it is not merely a question of Israel's individual or even corporate obedience to such private or social virtues as prayer, justice, kindness, and honesty. Israelites are expected to be faithful to their religion and its external forms of worship. So important is this requirement to Haggai that the Israelites must stop all other activities and "go up to the hills and bring wood and build the house" that is the temple of the Lord (Hag. 1:8).

Haggai adds an eschatological touch to Israel's rebuilding of the temple when he declares, in Yahweh's name, "that I may take pleasure in [the temple] and that I may appear [there] in my glory" (1:8). The Hebrew text for "appear in glory" implies a special moment when the weight of Yahweh's glorious presence will have a transforming effect in Israel. This passage is surcharged with some of the eschatological allusions of Ezekiel who spoke of the time when the glory of the Lord will fill the new temple, and from this temple there will flow a stream of fresh water to transform the Judean desert into a fertile paradise (Ezek. 43:1-5; 47:1-12).

A UNIQUE MOMENT OF TIME

The text in Hag. 1:2-4 is disturbed in the Hebrew, yet its reference to *time* is too important for Haggai's theology to overlook it:

> The people say *the time* has not yet come to rebuild the house of the LORD. . . . Is it *a time* for you yourselves to dwell in your paneled houses, while this house lies in ruins?

In fact, not twice but three times (in the Hebrew) Haggai introduces a special word for time ('et) which rarely if ever refers simply to an empty space of days or years. Rather, according to the study of Paul Neuenzeit, *Encyclopedia of Biblical Theology,* 911-15, time in biblical anthropology is always to be "filled *for* something." The action, moreover, filling each moment of time, is seen as completed or incompleted in the judgment of the speaker. Time is judged by its events, and these receive their significance in relation to the Lord's intention for them. The Lord decides how complete or incomplete the event turns out to be. There is, consequently, a special time for everything. Ecclesiastes plays effectively upon this sense of the word:

> A time for every matter under heaven:
> a time to be born, and a time to die;
> a time to plant, and a time to pluck up what is planted.
> (Eccl. 3:1-2)

Ps. 102:12-13 emphasizes the relationship not only between Israel and the chosen "time" but also the relationship between this moment and Yahweh's enthronement in the temple:

> But thou, O LORD, art enthroned for ever; . . .
> Thou wilt arise and have pity on Zion;
>   it is *the time* to favor her;
>   *the appointed time* has come.

While this "appointed time" brings special blessings to Israel, still other texts relate that particular moment to an extraordinary intervention of the Lord on the world scene:

> All the nations shall serve him [Nebuchadnezzar, king of Babylon] and his son and his grandson, until *the time* of his own

21

land comes; then many nations and great kings shall make him their slave (Jer. 27:7; cf. Isa. 13:22).

For Haggai *the time* of building the temple and of worship within it not only provides an opportunity for celebrating feasts on designated days of the year but it also prepares for the time of Yahweh's final blessing to come upon Israel from all corners of the world. Later in this prophecy, Haggai locates this eschatological intervention in the temple (Hag. 2:6-9).

Haggai is placing the same challenge and hope before us. We are not permitted simply to be good people in our private life; this goodness needs to be shared through church worship and public covenantal bonds. In this setting the glorious Lord Jesus will set an appointed time for the second coming.

THE IDENTITY OF THE "REMNANT"

In 1:12-14 Haggai definitely advances the theological meaning of the term *remnant*. His preaching on this theme will have serious, negative repercussions for the local people who never went into exile (see Introduction).

When this word first began to appear with the prophet Amos *ca.* 760 B.C., it designated those who may be left alive after a foreign invasion (Amos 5:14-15). So reduced are they to destitution, so caught up in pain and mourning in the city streets and countryside, there is question whether any chance of survival exists. Amos even compares them to bleeding pieces of a sheep, torn and mangled by lions (Amos 3:12). One rightly questions if anything alive can ever be reconstructed from this "remnant." Another prophet, contemporary for a while with Amos, though of a different background and pedigree, Isaiah by name, invests the word with more religious meaning and hope, this time including a mark of the Lord's special love. Isaiah names his older son Shear-jashub ("A remnant shall return," Isa. 7:3), a name that will be woven into the preaching of the prophecy and become an ever more important expression for hope after the Exile (Isa. 10:19-22; cf. Mic. 4:6-7). During the Exile "remnant" begins to refer to all Israel who will be redeemed and restored to their land (Isa. 46:3). After their restoration, however, the term takes on the restricted meaning of the returnees (Neh. 10:28-31; 11:1). This latter passage clearly distinguishes the returnees from the other local "peoples of the land," with whom the "true" Israelite was not to associate.

Haggai was a crucial person in limiting this word exclusively to those Israelites whose genealogy can be properly documented, from amongst those who returned from exile. Haggai stands in direct line with the prophet Ezekiel who was already rejecting those left behind in Jerusalem and favoring only those Israelites who were in exile (Ezek. 11:14-17; 33:29). Haggai, accordingly, strengthened those Jewish people who sided with Ezekiel and found the theology of Second Isaiah too open and liberal, especially as enunciated in the Servant Songs (cf. Isa. 42:4; 49:6) and repeated in the postexilic age by Third Isaiah (cf. 56:1-6; 66:18-23). The Isaian tradition, as it developed during and after the Exile, spoke of the light of Israel extending to the Gentiles and of some of them worshipping in the temple and even functioning there as priests.

For us today Haggai is a star biblical witness for the need of a sacred place for prayer and worship. He would not necessarily favor house churches, as we see them in the earliest days of Christianity (cf. 1 Cor. 11:17-22). To this extent he differs from many traditions in Deuteronomy with its recognition of prayer and instruction at home (Deut. 6:4-9, 20-25; 16:11). Haggai, moreover, recognized the need of clarity in religious teaching, not just in doctrine but equally as well in morality and even in community customs (Hag. 2:10-13). Haggai endorses distinct lines of authority in the community, the governor's and high priest's for rebuilding the temple (2:2), the other priests' for lesser questions (v. 11). Haggai may also be warning that self-identity is necessary but it can be carried too far, as happened later in postexilic Judah, for instance, when Ezra forced husbands to divorce and send away both wives and children if the wives were not of pure extraction from the families of the returnees (Ezra 10).

STIRRED BY THE SPIRIT

Again Haggai falls in line after Ezekiel, attributing the revival of Israel to *stirring up the spirit*. The spirit of the Lord featured prominently in early Israel after the settlement in the land. Elders performed their office of judge in settling domestic and community affairs through the inspiration of the spirit (Num. 11:10-30). Judges also led the army into battle, after the spirit of the Lord had rushed upon them and clothed them with strength (Judg. 6:34; 14:6). The prophetic bands were said to be possessed, or literally "conquered," by the spirit and so able to transform themselves into an ecstatic state, accomplish great wonders, and hardly be recognizable to themselves (cf. 1 Sam. 10:5-8). The classical prophets, however, beginning with Amos, avoided the use of the word. They had lost confidence in the authenticity of such ecstatic actions and did not want Israelites to excuse themselves from personal responsibility by placing total and exclusive confidence in Yahweh's marvelous intervention. Social justice towards the poor and powerless was far more important.

Isaiah begins the return to the use of "spirit" (Isa. 11). During the Exile, Second Isaiah makes a modest use of the word (Isa. 42:1; 44:3). In each case the spirit is no longer active in enabling people to accomplish superhuman feats of prowess. Rather, the spirit enables the servant to persevere silently, never snuffing out the faltering wick of fire nor breaking the bruised reed (Isa. 42:2-3), allowing God's blessings to continue with one's descendants like "willows by flowing streams" (Isa. 44:4). After the Exile, Third Isaiah frequently turns to this word, especially in such key passages as Isa. 61:1 for explaining his own call from the Lord, and 63:10-11 for perceiving the grief inflicted even upon God by our sins (see George A. F. Knight, *The New Israel,* 50-51). Ezekiel had brought the word back to a central place, as propounded by the early tradition in Judges and 1 Samuel. He revived within Israel the forceful intervention of the Spirit. In the vision of dry bones the four winds are summoned to sweep in and fit the bones together and cover them with sinew and flesh, breathing new life into them, so that they "stood upon their feet, an exceedingly great host" (Ezek. 37:1-10). Wind, breath, and spirit are identical words in the Hebrew.

With the verb "to stir up" in its causative mood, the action of the Spirit becomes all the more forceful. It is Yahweh who imparts mighty energy within such historical leaders as Cyrus the Great. The rhetorical question is asked in Isa. 41:2, "Who *stirred up* one from the east whom victory meets at every step?" and the affirmation is given in Isa. 42:13, "The LORD goes forth . . ., like a man of war he *stirs up* his fury." Haggai attributes the reconstruction of Israel, not like the earlier prophets to human works of social justice (Isa. 1), but to the mighty action of God's spirit.

Typical of Haggai, the work of the Spirit is concentrated on stirring up the people's enthusiasm for rebuilding the temple. In Haggai's judgment this action is as momentous as any heroic deed of the judges who were possessed by the Spirit (Judg. 6:34) or of Cyrus the Great (Isa. 41:2).

A SPLENDOR
GREATER THAN BEFORE
Haggai 1:15b–2:9

THE SPLENDOR OF THIS HOUSE

The prophecy of Haggai is leading up towards one of the two climaxes of his preaching, the announcement of the future elegance of the new temple and the contribution of the nations to its glory. The other climax in Hag. 2:20-23 centers upon Zerubbabel as messianic heir to the promises entrusted to the family of David. Particularly in the first instance Haggai carefully prepares the groundwork. The prophet continues with the same style, simple yet engaging, of questions, commands, repetitions, and divine promises, reaching even to what will seem humanly impossible for the people. He addresses not only Zerubbabel and Joshua, as in 1:1, but this time explicitly "all the remnant of the people." See the preceding section for a discussion of remnant.

The date and liturgical setting in 1:15b may have significantly influenced the prophet's preaching. (For 1:15a, see below.) It is the twenty-first day of the seventh month, i.e., 17 October 520. The Feast of Tabernacles would have been already celebrated, a feast that symbolized ever more emphatically God's kingdom in its final, eschatological glory (cf. Lev. 23:39-43; Neh. 8:9-18; Zech. 14:16-19). It is possible that the people would also have gathered at the beginning of this month for the New Year's festival (see Lev. 23:23-25) and that the Day of Atonement was also on their mind. Nehemiah 9:1 places *Yom Kippur* or the Day of Atonement only three days later on the twenty-fourth of this month. The high holy days always stir a strong sense of God's presence with the people of Israel and of God's intention to renew continuously the mighty acts of ancient times, celebrated in the liturgy. Deuteronomy 1–5, in fact, declares that each celebration is a new "today" for reexperiencing God's redemptive presence.

Important words or phrases from tradition enhance the seriousness of what Haggai is about to say. Three times Haggai supports and reaffirms the leaders and the people with the phrase, "Take

Courage!" Haggai recognizes that Israel is reliving a crucial period of time like that immediately after the death of Moses. Haggai's words are echoing the Lord's commissioning of Moses' successor, Joshua, as he was about to lead Israel across the Jordan to take possession of their promised land (Josh. 1:6, 7, 9, 18). Now that the Exile is over and Israel is resettling the land, the task in this new day included, as it did in former times, *work* on the temple. The climactic sentence in this new commissioning is: *"Work,* for I am with you, says the LORD of hosts, according to the promise that I made you when you came out of Egypt" (Hag. 2:4-5). Haggai then repeats another word, prominent in the commissioning of Joshua: "Fear not!" (Josh. 1:5-7, 9).

Haggai strengthens the governor, the high priest, and the people with this assurance from the Lord: "My Spirit abides among you." For *Spirit,* see 1:14. The Hebrew for *abide* is translated with a variety of words in English and connotes at times a ceremonial or religious act, as when the high priest Joshua was *"standing* before the angel of the LORD" (Zech. 3:1), or when the prophet Elijah was expected to "stand and call on the name of the LORD" (2 Kgs. 5:11). A variation of the same word denoted *the cloud* that led Israel through the desert (Exod. 13:21) and that "filled the house of the LORD" at the time of its consecration by King Solomon (1 Kgs. 8:10). Haggai's language is consistently traditional, cultic, and centering upon the new temple.

The statement in Hag. 2:6a, "Once again, in a little while," clearly designates an important event on the immediate horizon. The rebuilding of the temple was leading Israel quickly to the verge of an eschatological finale, a total fulfillment of promises. The ancient Greek text, however, reads differently. Changing "in a little while" to read "yet once more," the translator shifted the emphasis from the imminent future within everyone's lifetime to a new and unknown moment in the distant future. Very possibly when the glorious finale did not quickly burst with splendor upon Israel, the Greek translator adapted the text to the necessity of waiting for still another time, "yet once more." This Greek reading will be employed to advantage by Heb. 12:26-28 to claim that the Second Temple of Haggai's time was to be replaced "yet once more" by a new kind of temple in the person of the glorified, resurrected Jesus. It is this new, spiritual temple that can never be shaken:

> This phrase, "Yet once more," indicates the removal of what is shaken, . . . in order that what cannot be shaken may remain.

Therefore let us be grateful for receiving a kingdom that cannot be shaken, and thus let us offer to God acceptable worship, with reverence and awe (Heb. 12:27-28).

Returning to Haggai's times, we find another idea, different from that in the Epistle to the Hebrews, intended in the phrase, "*I will shake* the heavens and the earth and the sea and the dry land; and *I will shake* all nations" (Hag. 2:6-7). Haggai may easily have been prompted to think of the many revolts that convulsed the Persian Empire upon the death of Cambyses in 522 (see Introduction). Yet these military actions by warring, jealous, and power-hungry factions within the Persian Empire will not accomplish the divine will for Israel. Grammatically the Hebrew stresses that it is "I, Yahweh" who will act. Haggai, therefore, is not encouraging civil revolts but bases Israel's hope exclusively on what Yahweh will accomplish through the divine presence in the temple. Haggai's theology has a solid base in political reality, yet its message is not a call for political action but a call for faithful waiting upon the Lord. It would have been disastrous, moreover, for tiny Yehud, as the country of Israel is now called, to take sides in the massive power struggle in the Persian Empire.

The word *shake* (Hebrew *r'sh*) evokes many memories: the shaking of Mount Sinai when Yahweh bestowed the law (Exod. 19:18); the holy wars to achieve control of the promised land (Judg. 5:4); the liturgical celebration of the settlement in the land (Ps. 68:8). The new age will be greater than the old, as Haggai declares:

> The latter splendor of this house shall be greater than the former, says the Lord of hosts; and in this place I will give prosperity, says the Lord of hosts. (2:9)

At the same time the new is intimately linked with the old. The new, in the thinking of Haggai, does more than repeat tradition; it builds upon it. In the same way the Greek translator of Haggai and the author of the Epistle to the Hebrews quote the words of Haggai, yet they too lead the sense of Haggai's prophecy into a new kind of fulfillment. New Testament quotations generally present the OT, first in accord with an interpretation evolving from the rabbis and the Greek translators, and second in the excelling light of the revelation of the resurrected and glorious Jesus.

Finally the phrase in v. 7 that "the treasures of the nations shall come in" not only manifests the eschatological thinking of Haggai but also prepares for a new messianic interpretation in the Christian

Scriptures. Textual difficulties in the Hebrew and variations among the ancient versions have even helped to heighten the messianic meaning. Grammatically, the Hebrew has a singular subject and a plural verb; the Greek, a plural subject and a singular verb! Jerome transformed the singular neuter "it," the subject in the Hebrew text, into a personal noun, meaning "the Desired One [or Messiah] of all the nations." This text will receive its fulfillment when the Messiah enters this temple. If we link the passage with other similar ones, like Isa. 2:2-4 and 60:6-9 which envisage the nations streaming to Jerusalem to offer gifts to Yahweh, then the RSV translation in the neuter plural, "the treasures of all nations," is preferable for appreciating the original sense of Haggai's preaching. In any case, Haggai foresees a glory and a wealth for this new temple that far surpasses Solomon's temple.

FROM THE SECULAR TO THE SACRED

By faith and by a firm anchoring in tradition Haggai recognizes in his own time a repetition of Israel's history and especially of God's wondrous actions within it. He also perceives God's active presence within the secular events of his own time, like the conquest of Babylon by Cyrus the Great, the permission from Cyrus for all conquered people, including the Israelites, to return to their own land, and the revolts that racked the Persian Empire at the death of Cambyses. From the viewpoint of world history the second of these events, allowing the Israelites to return to their homeland, was quite insignificant, hardly worthy of a place in the annals of Persia and Egypt, whatever be its pivotal and transforming force for Israel. It would have seemed ridiculous braggadocio to assume that world history revolved around the ten to twenty thousand Israelites who returned poor and disspirited from Babylonian captivity. Cyrus' edict, allowing all captives to reestablish themselves in their homeland, was part of his international program for peace and strength in his newly won empire. Israel may have been one of the least important of these groups, even if it is one of the only to survive in our historical annals.

For an event to become historical, more is necessary than the mere fact that it happened. Most of reality never becomes history. History, moreover, turns events into a force for world significance for reasons other than the fact that they took place. History, therefore, always includes more than details and always, albeit implicitly, stresses the meaning and impact of the event more than the actual event itself.

Events from the early days of Israel could easily have been forgotten, had they not been preserved and celebrated in the liturgy. Because the exodus out of Egypt was commemorated as "a memorial feast" at the Jerusalem temple and other sanctuaries, each new generation was drawn into the experience of the event. The worshippers recognized how Yahweh was leading them out of their own kind of oppression and need (Exod. 12:14, 26-27; Deut. 6:20-25). Liturgical celebrations from one generation to another transformed insignificant events into salvation history for Israel and sometimes into world history for other peoples as well. As mentioned already in the Introduction, because Israel liturgically celebrated the Exodus, even a godless nation such as Soviet Russia must deal with the people and the country Israel today.

Liturgy does more than insert small, secular events into the annals of history. Liturgy highlights the active presence of God among the chosen people of faith. While liturgy is creating history, its purpose is not history but worship that centers upon a personal, omnipotent God engaged in redeeming the chosen people Israel. The liturgical action focused upon God immediately present in the moment of worship, and through this religious action left its important mark upon secular history.

The new temple, accordingly, revitalized the past and prepared for the final, glorious fulfillment. Haggai recognized the necessity of: (1) realistically accepting the turns and twists of world events; (2) perceiving the hand of Yahweh extended within these events, "shak[ing] the heavens and the earth . . . and all nations" for Israel's salvation; and (3) drawing upon tradition and especially liturgical practice for the language and ceremony of remembrance.

THE TREASURES OF ALL NATIONS

The nations contribute not only the stage setting of world events but also their "treasures" of silver and gold for the realization of Yahweh's promises to Israel:

> For thus says the LORD of hosts: Once again, in a little while, I will shake the heavens and the earth and the sea and the dry land; and I will shake all nations, so that the treasures of all nations shall come in, and I will fill this house with splendor, says the LORD of hosts. The silver is mine, and the gold is mine,

says the LORD of hosts. The latter splendor of this house shall
be greater than the former, says the LORD of hosts (2:6-9a).

Haggai is saying first of all that the flow of the treasures of the nations to the temple is to be attributed to the same divine action that
leads to the reestablishment of the temple. Haggai employs the same
verb, "shake," of the impact of God's purpose in the heavens and the
earth, across sea and dry land, now to the contribution of all the nations whom "I will shake." Without the nations Israel alone cannot
rebuild the temple and be ready for the messianic moment. This supreme moment of the Scriptures is a joint venture of Israel and the
nations.

As in the days of David and Solomon, so now the nations' treasures consist of more than material resources, even though the text
mentions only silver and gold. In Israel's history the nations con-
tributed such cultural achievements as architectural styles, musical
instruments, and melodies for singing (1 Kgs. 4–5), titles for addressing Yahweh, and consequently insights into the mysteries of
faith (Ps. 29; 48:1-8; 89:5-13).

If the achievements among the nations assist in rebuilding the
temple and in adorning Israel's worship within the temple, then a
further question arises: Do the nations have *a rightful place* within
the temple and within Israel's worship? Some prophets, perhaps
contemporaneous with Haggai, who belong to the school or dis-
cipleship of Second Isaiah and continue the exilic prophet's message
in the homeland after the Exile, will answer the question with an emphatic and repeated "Yes!" (Isa. 56:6; 61:6; 66:18-21). As will be
evident in Haggai's next speech (Hag. 2:10-14), this prophet never
developed the intuition or outreach towards the nations. He even
pulled back from it and restricted Israel's relationship with its half-
gentile, half-Jewish neighbors, a people later to be called the Samaritans. Yet the intuition is there in the text of his preaching for future
generations to develop.

Strangely and even cruelly enough, in another shaking of the
heavens and the earth, the nations will intervene again, destroying
this temple built at the insistent urging of Haggai. This new setting
for the text will come in NT times. The Epistle to the Hebrews
quotes Haggai's words, but according to the ancient Greek reading,
to explain how the world was to be shaken "yet once more" in the
death of Jesus and in the destruction of Jerusalem and its temple by
the Romans. To understand the text from Hebrews we turn first to

Matthew's gospel, which associates the rending of the temple veil with the death of Jesus:

> And Jesus cried again with a loud voice and yielded up his spirit. And behold, the curtain of the temple was torn in two, from top to bottom; and the earth shook, and the rocks were split; the tombs also were opened, and many bodies of the saints who had fallen asleep were raised. (Matt. 27:50-52)

Matthew is indicating either that God has abandoned the Jerusalem temple, depriving it of its sacredness and condemning it to destruction (cf. Ezek. 10:18-19), or else that the temple was now open to the world. Elsewhere in his gospel Matthew combines the two tragic moments of Jesus' death and the temple's demolition (Matt. 24). The Epistle to the Hebrews develops some of the theological implications. The rending of the temple veil is associated with the opening of the heart of Jesus by the soldier's spear (John 19:34):

> We have confidence to enter the sanctuary by the blood of Jesus, by the new and living way which he opened for us through the curtain, that is, through his flesh. (Heb. 10:19-20)

The heart of Jesus becomes a new temple of worship where Jesus is "the mediator of a new covenant" (Heb. 12:24) and the supreme high priest (Heb. 4:14; 10:21). Here men and women of every race are invited to enter.

The temple tradition was thus realized not in a temple made by hands (Mark 14:58; Acts 7:48-50) but in Jesus' glorious body (John 2:19-21) together with all the members of Christ's body (Eph. 2:20-22; 1 Pet. 2:4-7). The stones of the Jerusalem temple, put into place at the urging of Haggai, become symbolic of the bonding of Christians with one another in adoration before and even within the risen and glorified Jesus.

> Come to him [the Lord Jesus], to that living stone, rejected by men but in God's sight chosen and precious; and like living stones be yourselves built into a spiritual house, to be a holy priesthood, to offer spiritual sacrifices acceptable to God through Jesus Christ. (1 Pet. 2:4-5)

This fulfillment of prophecy is shattering to what Haggai understood by his own words, yet all the while it is implicit within the prophet's statement. Haggai was insisting that the rebuilding of the material temple was crucial for the survival of Israel and for the coming of the final age of the world. And he was right! He recognized the role of the nations and the shaking of the universe in the glory of the messianic temple. The NT shifts the promises centering in temple symbolically to Jesus and Christian believers. Like Haggai it introduces world-shattering events that lead to the completion of the hopes for the temple. Admittedly, the NT takes advantage of a reinterpretation of Haggai within the Greek LXX, which saw the fulfillment not "in a little while" but "yet once more" in a new shaking of the heavens and the earth.

From this example we see that prophecy can provide practical decisions for the present moment and strengthen one's faith in seeking the future, but it does not always dictate the exact details of future fulfillment. In fact, in that completion of the sacred word God will continue to take us by surprise (cf. Isa. 48:3; Mal. 3:1).

CLEANLINESS AND BLESSINGS
Haggai 2:10-19 (+ 1:15a)

PRIESTLY DECISION, PROPHETICALLY REINTERPRETED

As a preface to what follows, we draw attention to the textual difficulty at 1:15–2:1. Two sets of dates follow immediately upon each other:

> 1:15a   On the twenty-fourth day of the month, in the sixth month.
>
> 1:15b–2:1   In the second year of Darius the king, in the seventh month, on the twenty-first day of the month, the word of the LORD came by Haggai the prophet.

We follow the suggestion of scholars that the speech of Haggai that was originally introduced by 1:15a was relocated by the editor to 2:10-19. The editor had a reason for this dislocation, and the reason contained a religious message for a later audience.

Two inspired speakers/writers, therefore, each made their complementary yet separate contribution to the book of Haggai. First and basic is Haggai, the *prophet-preacher,* who was uniquely responsible for the people's return to the task of rebuilding the temple and for their separation from the local population who never went into exile. Second and supplementary is the *editor* who organized the latter's sermons to maintain a prophetic challenge for a later generation and to accentuate the messianic oracles in 2:2-9 and 2:20-23. As mentioned in the Introduction, the editor gave the book its larger structure (see above, 15, for the overall plan, according to Théophane Chary, *Aggée—Zacharie Malachie,* 12). The editor, therefore, shifted 2:15-19 from its original place immediately after 1:15a, and in doing so, has adapted the meaning of Haggai's statement in 2:10-14. He also left 1:15a hanging without any context. The RSV, for its part, associates 1:15a with the preceding section as its conclusion, a very unusual place in Haggai for dates. The editor helped to stitch the oracle that originally followed 1:15a into its new place by the repetition of the identical Hebrew phrase, "all the work of their [or your] hands" in vv. 14 and 17. The latter is translated in the RSV as "all the products of your toil."

Originally Haggai's preaching in 2:10-14 would have declared unclean those local inhabitants who had not been taken into exile, including the people in the former northern kingdom, eventually to be named the "Samaritans." By attaching vv. 15-19 to the preceding section, the editor shifted the focus away from these "people of the land" to the returnees, declaring the latter to be just as unclean as the former group and their work on the temple just as unacceptable if they do not repent. The editor announces that temple rebuilding is not sufficient. Unlike the prophet Zechariah, no other requirements are placed on the people's conscience. We miss the usual prophetic defense of social justice (cf. Zech. 7:8-10).

According to this hypothesis, originally proposed by Ernst Sellin in 1900-1901 (*Studien* 2:50ff), vv. 15-19 originally belonged immediately after 1:15a and was spoken on "the twenty-fourth day of the . . . sixth month," 21 September 520, while the date at 2:10 places vv. 10-14 on "the twenty-fourth day of the ninth month," 18 December 520. Although we follow this explanation here, we also recognize serious difficulties: (1) Haggai otherwise never mentions the Samaritans, but in response we can say that his association in thought with Ezekiel and the Chronicler would support his antagonism to the local inhabitants (Ezek. 6; 11:14-21; Ezra 4:1-6); (2) the date in Hag. 2:18 corresponds with 2:10, not with 1:15a, but in response the former verse can be the editor's work.

Another support for some editorial changes comes from the textual problems here. The shifting of sections from one place to another frequently enough results in textual unevenness. Haggai 2:14 has a long addition in the ancient Greek version: "on account of their early burdens; they shall be pained because of their toils; and you have hated them who reprove [you] at the gates"—referring to Israel's antagonism to prophetic warnings. Verse 17, "Yet you did not return to me," is a correction of the Hebrew text, drawn from Amos 4:9, which speaks of many natural and political disasters, sent by the Lord that Israel might reform its ways. Haggai 2:19 is "the most difficult verse in Haggai" (Douglas R. Jones, *Haggai, Zechariah and Malachi,* 52), for it can be explained either that the land is already bearing fruit or that the people are questioning that it ever will, implying the answer, "No!" The prophet immediately adds this assurance from the Lord: "From this day on I will bless you."

CLEANLINESS AND ELECTION

In vv. 10-14 Haggai reflects an entirely new attitude in prophecy by referring to the priests the question: When and how do objects become clean or unclean? Up till now prophets never even considered such questions, nor do we have any instance among prophets of submitting inquiries to priests. Haggai accepts the strict laws of clean and unclean as elaborated in the Priestly tradition of the Pentateuch (Lev. 11–16). These laws reflect hygiene, custom, and social standards as well as moral and religious norms. As Mary Douglas has written (*Purity and Danger,* 41-57), Israel's laws of cleanness and wholeness depend on standards that evolved over many centuries of what was considered normal and acceptable to the majority of people in a given society. Even in the modern society of the Western world, a set of rules for cleanliness or acceptability are firmly in place. For instance, a person's foot may be cleaner than his or her hand, yet it is "unclean" to place this foot upon the dinner table. It is equally "unclean" to greet a person in one's home barefoot. Yet in another country, it may be equally "unclean" to wear shoes within the home. A disabled person without arms may use legs and feet with grace and dexterity at the dinner table—only to be considered unclean! What is acceptable or unacceptable in society extends to rules of modesty and toilet habits. It applies to every aspect of life, if one considers it seriously.

In Leviticus this interpretation of what is clean or unclean applies to all forms of living creatures. The basic principle derives from what is considered normal. Fish, accordingly, without scales and fins do not conform to the law of normal behavior for fish and so are unclean. The same principle has to do with human beings. A person with a physical disability (i.e., one who cannot walk on two legs but needs some other kind of locomotion) is "unclean" and barred from full participation in society (Lev. 21:16-23). These rules are extended to foreigners even by the otherwise more lenient text of Deuteronomy (cf. Deut. 23:2-9; Neh. 13:1-3); for a contrary, more open position, see Isa. 56:1-8. Foreigners are generally considered strange—in biblical language "unclean"—because their norms of regular behavior as regards food, dress, and etiquette have developed differently.

The levitical rules of cleaniness and holiness were revised and codified during the Exile under the influence of Ezekiel. Those Israelites who were not taken into exile but had remained behind in the land never had the opportunity to participate in the serious effort at reforming and enforcing the Mosaic laws during the Exile. Perhaps even unknowingly they allowed themselves to become "unclean." There is good reason to think that the priests' decision in Haggai is directed against these local people. Haggai thus explains the priests' decision:

> So is it with this people, and with this nation before me, says the LORD; and so with every work of their hands; and what they offer there is unclean. (2:14)

Haggai marks the beginning of a serious rift between the returnees and the local "people of the land *('am ha'arets)*." These latter, who originated from many different sources, will eventually rally together against the "Jews" and form their own separate group called "Samaritans."

Haggai stands as an important person in reenforcing Israel's stringent rules of separateness. At certain historical moments God's people, if they are to survive, must close ranks and clearly identify themselves. Such action means that they see themselves to be different and separate from others.

Haggai also enunciates the common experience that evil is more contagious than goodness. "Holy flesh," carried in the skirt of one's garment, the priests inform the questioner in 2:10-14, does not render anything it touches holy, but if one is unclean by reason of touching a corpse, anything touched by such a person automatically becomes unclean. If we apply this principle to moral influence, it may be said that evil's influence can be detected and gauged far more accurately than virtue's.

AFFIRMATION
OF DAVIDIC RULE
Haggai 2:20-23

Haggai is speaking "a second time . . . on the twenty-fourth day of the [ninth] month," namely 18 December 520 (see 2:10). Typical of Haggai's style, the section here is replete with words and phrases from Israel's repertoire of liturgical celebrations, priestly statements, and prophetic preaching.

The book of Haggai concludes with a final oracle focusing upon the Davidic heir, Zerubbabel. We find not only the editor's customary introduction in v. 20, but also a very solemn final statement in v. 23, thrice declaring in the form of a prophetic revelation: "says the LORD" *(ne'um yhwh)*. While the first half of the book, as put together by the editor (1:1–2:9), reaches a climax in an oracle about the future "messianic" glory of the *temple,* the second half confides the glory of the temple to the *Davidic dynasty.* This family is said to exert a decisive role in the messianic future. As yet, Zerubbabel and the dynasty had not yet been eclipsed by the high priest Joshua and the temple priesthood (cf. Zech. 6:9-14).

God's determination to "shake the heavens and the earth" in the rebuilding of the temple (see 2:6-7) is now closely tied with Zerubbabel. The restoration of the Davidic dynasty and the defeat of the nations (v. 22) are announced in the style of the Song of Moses celebrating the exodus out of Egypt (Exod. 15:1-18) and of Second Isaiah's victory song of the new Exodus (Isa. 43:16-17). Language of the "holy war" echoes here from the books of Joshua and Judges. Another phrase about the "overthrow . . . of kingdoms" (Hag. 2:22) resonates with the fearful quaking of the earth at the collapse of Sodom and Gemorrah in Gen. 19:21-29 (cf. Ezek. 38:18-23). The final words in Hag. 2:22, they "shall go down, every one by the sword of his fellow," seem a later addition. They disrupt whatever poetic rhythm might be detected in Haggai; they also break the scenario of Yahweh's exclusive activity, indicated by the language of the holy war. Attention is turned instead to human military efforts.

As mentioned already, Haggai was not a political revolutionary but an eschatologist, stressing the Lord's exclusive part in fulfilling Israel's hopes. Temple liturgy that focused upon the Lord's immediate, active presence in renewing the great deeds of the past became an ideal ambience for expressing this religious attitude.

In v. 23 every phrase is heavy with messianic meaning. The opening words, "on that day," link Haggai's oracle here with a long tradition that is not only liturgical (Deut. 5:1-5, 22-30; Ps. 118:24) but is found as well among the prophets (Zeph. 1:14-16; Isa. 10:20; 11:10). At first it was a day of dark destruction on account of sin; later it was announced as a day of renewal on account of the Lord's mercy, to be celebrated in the sanctuary. The phrase, "I will take you," evokes other memories of a strong action on Yahweh's part, like taking Enoch (or Henoch) and Elijah from this earth (Gen. 5:21-24; 2 Kgs. 2:1-5), as well as the Lord's choice of prophets (Amos 7:15) and kings (2 Sam. 7:8). The same Hebrew word *(laqah)* occurs in each case.

Zerubbabel is next designated "my servant," a title that declares a close bond of collaboration and dialogue with the Lord. It is bestowed upon kings (2 Sam. 7:5; Ps. 132:10), upon prophets (Isa. 42:1), and upon prophetic communities (Isa. 41:8; 63:17). It is addressed to those foreigners invited to become members of the prophetic community (Isa. 56:6) and to Nebuchadnezzar, the Lord's special agent (Jer. 27:6). Zerubbabel, furthermore, is compared to the Lord's "signet ring," a precious object worn on a finger (Gen. 41:42; Esth. 3:10) or hung from the neck (Gen. 38:18, 25) and used to impress an official seal upon documents (Jer. 32:9-44). Zerubbabel was to place the seal of his signet ring upon the events of this age by furthering the reconstruction of the temple. Thus he authenticated the Lord's decision for all future generations of Israelites to see. Finally, the Lord pronounced the oracle over Zerubbabel: "I have chosen you," so that the long history of Israel's election is concentrated in this descendant of King David.

Haggai's hopes for temple and for dynasty never came literally true. His statement about the temple as the place where "in a little while" God's messianic glory will be revealed, far more gloriously than anything in preexilic days (Hag. 2:8), had to be revised, as we saw in the Greek translation of the LXX. "A little while" is extended into a long period of time, leading "yet once again" to a different age. His plans for the Davidic dynasty were quickly put aside as the high priest took over the role of civil leadership. This transition we will study in chs. 3 and 6 of Zechariah. Prophecy, therefore, addresses the hopes to be sustained at any given moment according to the political, economic, and religious needs. Prophecy never separates religion from such realities. By sustaining hopes prophecy enables the community to continue into a new age that brings its own set of problems and possibilities.

It is not that truth changes. Rather, the pastoral application of truth modulates, so that the essential religious kernel can be distinguished from cultural and other conditional factors. This kernel never appears by itself, so that every expression needs new refinement in any new age. The presence of Jesus as Messiah was an exceptionally all new aspect and imparts an extraordinarily clear focus upon the kernel. Yet even NT writers are conditioned by their times and circumstances. Each age learns new aspects about temple and leadership as about clean and unclean. For OT people this new learning was always in accord with the insights of the Mosaic covenant; for Christians it is in the light of Jesus Christ. Prophecy is the bridge, not only from religion to the moral, political problems of its own age, but also from the religious solutions of an earlier age to the needs of the later age. While tradition is the line of survival, prophecy enables it to be worthy of survival.

CONCLUSION TO
THE BOOK OF HAGGAI

Haggai, in two short chapters, in a ministry of less than four months, and in four or five short sermons, combines extraordinary gifts:

(1) a strong attachment to tradition, especially as this has been transmitted through the southern sources of ancient Jerusalem and the exilic prophet Ezekiel, and an unwillingness to diverge from it unless under a clear sign from the Lord;

(2) an unusual devotion to the temple and its liturgy, as well as a loyal recognition of the Davidic heir, Zerubbabel;

(3) a practical sense of what can be accomplished and how it ought to be urged in clear, prosaic language;

(4) a strong momentum, at least from the editor, leading twice to Israel's "messianic" future, in the temple and in the royal Davidic line;

(5) a sense of God's plans as these work their way towards fulfillment amid world politics. The heavens and the earth are shaken in the revolts within the Persian Empire, yet Haggai advocates a nonpolitical or at least a non-military solution to Israel's problems and messianic hopes. Through the use of the language of the holy war, Haggai focuses almost exclusively upon the Lord's activity in dedicating the nations and their treasures to the temple and in reestablishing Davidic rule.

This blend of the old and the new, of prophecy and priesthood, of politics and religion, leaning always towards priesthood, religion, and the new, made Haggai one of the only successful prophets in the Hebrew Scriptures. Judging from our documents, we can acclaim this prophet as *the* most responsible person for Israel's survival in the traumatic transition from exile to resettlement in its own land.

Despite these small but significant successes, the next prophet, Zechariah, will be forced by circumstances to reverse the emphasis away from Zerubbabel and focus it ever more exclusively upon the high priest, Joshua, and the temple liturgy. Prophecy, therefore, combines a strong sense of decisive action for its own contemporary moment with a more general and more lasting faith in the messianic future. Biblical interpretation always faces the difficult task of distinguishing what is passing from what is enduring for all generations—even if the "passing" details seemed most important at the time. Sometimes the lasting "kernel" appears only as a flashing signal, left undeveloped by the original prophet, elaborated on at a later time by another of God's servants. For example, Haggai in his comments about the role of the nations in 2:6-9 only hints at what assumes a central place in NT theology (cf. Heb. 12:26-29 and the discussion of Hag. 2:6-9). As mentioned in the opening statement of this book, prophecy has its history, in which each biblical age made its own divinely inspired contribution.

A Commentary on the Book of
Zechariah

CONTENTS

THE PROPHECY OF
ZECHARIAH, CHS. 1–8

INTRODUCTION

The book of Zechariah is not only the longest in the collection of the twelve minor prophets but it has other important claims to distinction. Of all the OT books it stands out as the one most quoted in the Gospel narrative of the passion, death, and resurrection of Jesus (Paul Lamarche, *Zacharie IX–XIV,* 8-9). Every study, therefore, of messianism and the fulfillment of prophecy in the NT must give considerable attention to Zechariah.

This concern has been bestowed upon a book that according to general consensus is one of the most obscure in the Bible (Ralph L. Smith, *Micah–Malachi,* 166-67). At times the problems of interpretation come from the imperfect condition of some key passages in the Hebrew text (e.g., Zech. 6:9-14; 12:10), at other times from the editorial replacement of verses. The editor inserted passages such as 4:6-10 and 13:7-9 for a special purpose, yet they break the continuity of the prophet's original preaching and are transferred elsewhere (to their original place?) in some translations of the Bible (see chs. 3-4 in the NAB). Other difficulties arise in the book of Zechariah from vague points of reference (e.g., identity of the shepherds in 11:4-17) or from the highly symbolic nature of visionary writing (e.g., the vision of the woman in the ephah [5:5-11]).

Political crises may have added their own set of questions for the modern reader: e.g., the disappearance of Zerubbabel, governor of the land by Persian appointment and the last representative of the Davidic line in a position of authority. In 3:6-10 his power and privileges as governor are subsumed by the high priest, even though attempts are made in other places of the book of Zechariah to reassert the role of the Davidic heir. Lines originally about Zerubbabel are inserted into passages dealing with both high priest and governor (4:6-10) or about the high priest alone (6:12-13). Obscure, tantalizing references to the royal family of David reappear in the second part of Zechariah (9:9-10; ch. 12).

Chapters 1–8 are being treated separately as the work of "First Zechariah," the original prophet who was a contemporary of the

46

prophet Haggai. His preaching and writing were collated and edited by the first of his disciples; his prophetic mantle was handed down to still other disciples of a much later age. These latter were responsible for chs. 9–14, as will be discussed in the separate introduction to these chapters. In the course of this commentary we will speak simply of "Zechariah." If the context is chs. 9–14, we always mean the later disciple(s), at times called "Second Zechariah." Some scholars will subdivide chs. 9–14 into Second and Third Zechariah (chs. 9–11; 12–14), just as the book of Isaiah is frequently divided between First Isaiah (chs. 1–39), Second Isaiah (chs. 40–55) and Third Isaiah (chs. 56–66). Chapters 9 and 12 of Zechariah and chapter 1 of Malachi are each introduced in the Hebrew with the title *massa'*, which the RSV and the NAB translate as "Oracle" and the JPSV as "pronouncement." We are speaking, therefore, of an inspired tradition of Isaiah or Zechariah rather than of a single inspired author. These two prophets, as they appear in the text of the Bible, are more than individuals, moved by the spirit to pronounce the word of God; they become a school of thought or a religious movement. They continued to exist in their disciples, who kept their message alive in new circumstances amid a new set of questions and opportunities. The charism of prophetic inspiration is contagious (cf. 1 Sam. 10:5-7); the mantle of one prophet falls upon the shoulders of disciples, and others exclaim: "The spirit of Elijah rests on Elisha" (2 Kgs. 2:15).

The character of the original prophet with the name of Zechariah is hidden within the lines of chs. 1–8; we turn now to search out this person.

THE PERSON OF ZECHARIAH

The author is introduced as "Zechariah the son of Berechiah, son of Iddo, the prophet." Zechariah is a common enough name in the Hebrew Bible and poses little or no problem; it means "Yahweh remembers," from the Hebrew word *zakar*, "to remember," followed by the suffix "Yah" or "Yahweh." Persons with this name are listed at least thirty-three times in the Hebrew Bible, and almost half of them belong to the tribe of Levi, at times to the priestly family of Aaron (cf. Theodor M. Mauch, *IDB* 4:941-43; see also Olivier Odelain and Raymond Seguineau, *Dictionary of Proper Names and Places in the Bible*, 394-95).

Problems arise in trying to identify Berechiah and Iddo. Ezra 5:1; 6:14 refer to "Haggai and Zechariah the son of Iddo," omitting any reference to Berechiah. Around 500 B.C. Iddo was included among the twenty priestly families (cf. Neh. 12:16). Long before the Exile Isaiah spoke of a person with the name of "Zechariah the son of Jeberechiah" (Isa. 8:2). The Greek Septuagint for Isa. 8:2 shortens the name of Jeberechiah to Berechiah. Some writers like Ernst Sellin, Matthias Delcor, Friedrich Horst, and Otto Eissfeldt offer the hypothesis that the name of "Zechariah son of Berechiah" from Isa. 8:2 was first attached to Haggai 9–14, so that each section of the prophecy, chs. 1–8 and 9-14, could be identified with a person by the name of Zechariah. This background or parentage through Berechiah was then absorbed into the genealogy of "Zechariah son of Iddo" in 1:1 (cf. Théophane Chary, *Aggée—Zacharie Malachie*, 38).

The confusion continues in the reference of Matt. 23:35 to a "Zechariah the son of Barachiah, whom you murdered between the sanctuary and the altar." Matthew is most probably alluding to still another "Zechariah the son of Jehoiada the priest [who was] stoned [to death] in the the court of the house of the LORD" by order of King Joash (2 Chr. 24:20-22). The Targum or Aramaic translation of Lam. 2:20, "Should priest and prophet be slain in the sanctuary of the LORD?" identifies this person as Zechariah, son of Iddo (H. G. T. Mitchell, *Haggai, Zechariah,* 83). There is a marked tendency for the more important Zechariah, author of chs. 1–8, to absorb the activities of other, lesser known Zechariahs. Again, as discussed in the preceding section, "Zechariah" turns out to be more than an inspired individual; we do better to speak of an inspired Zechariah tradition.

The presence of Zechariah and Haggai is further enhanced in the Greek Septuagint, the Syriac, and the Latin Vulgate, which attribute various psalms to these prophets.

In any case, the exact identity of Zechariah is the first of many historical problems in this prophecy. We are reminded that while the Bible rests firmly upon God's actions within the history of Israel, its purpose is not historical but theological and pastoral. In the oral transmission of religious traditions, as even today in sermons, historical details can be blended together for the sake of an overall moral or instructional impact upon the contemporary audience.

There is no doubt that two prophets, named Haggai and Zechariah, prophesied between 520 and 517. Further details about family and genealogy and the relation to other persons in the Bible with the name Zechariah are left uncertain.

ZECHARIAH, PRIEST AND PROPHET

Zechariah's association with a priestly family emerges not only from his interest in temple and priesthood but also from the various allusions in his preaching to the two books of Chronicles, a priestly document par excellence. There is precedent for this combination of priest and prophet. Jeremiah came from a priestly family of Anathoth (Jer. 1:1) while Ezekiel too was a priest (Ezek. 1:3). Zechariah shows up more closely aligned to the southern priestly type of Ezekiel and is more sympathetic towards the Jerusalem temple than to priests like Jeremiah of a northern background. These latter had been exiled from Jerusalem to Anathoth by Solomon (cf. 1 Kgs. 2:26-27) and remained antagonistic to the temple (cf. Jer. 7 and 26).

The priest Zechariah was very concerned about the purity not only of the temple (Zech. 5:1-4, 5-11) but also of the high priest (ch. 3). In fact purity reaches into all areas of the people's lives through the ritual cleansing and reconsecration of the high priest (ch. 3). While the prophecy of Haggai ends with a focus upon Zerubbabel the governor, the prophecy of Zechariah gradually eliminates Zerubbabel in favor of the high priest. The sanctuary is ever more clearly the center of messianic fulfillment (1:16; 4:9; 6:12-13), and in Second Zechariah it is a messianic sanctuary without any presence at all of the Davidic messiah (cf. ch. 14).

The *prophetic* side of Zechariah's character, however, shows up ever more distinctly than the priestly and tends to dominate chs. 1–8. This aspect of Zechariah's character is clear enough, not only from his being numbered among the twelve minor prophets and because of his eloquent prophetical sermons, especially in ch. 7, but also because of the editor's anxiety to link Zechariah with the "former prophets" (1:4-6; 7:7, 12; 8:9). Zechariah is more fluent than Haggai in weaving texts or memories of earlier prophets into his preaching. We think of the allusions to the "seventy years" of Jeremiah (cf. Jer. 25:11; 29:10 and Zech. 1:12; 7:5), and of Second Isaiah's comfort for Zion (Isa. 51:3 and Zech. 1:17). The call for "Silence!" in 2:13 reminds us of Hab. 2:20, and the notion of a "brand plucked from the fire" in Zech. 3:2 comes from Amos 4:11. Zechariah was at ease with prophetic language.

Zechariah's penchant for communicating with God and with fellow Israelites through dreams corresponds with a long prophetic tradition. Dreams show up in that section of the Pentateuch called the Elohist, e.g., in the dreams of Abimelech (Gen. 20:3) and of

Joseph (Gen. 37). The Elohist section is also appreciative of prophecy, as we see in the account of Balaam the seer or prophet (Num. 22-24) and in the understanding of the elders as prophets (Num. 12:24-30). Dreams, moreover, or at least visions occupy an important place in the call of the prophet Amos (Amos 7:1-9; 8:1-3; 9:1-6). Angels that assist Zechariah in understanding his dreams are also on hand for Ezekiel (Ezek. 40:3-4). A scroll, seen in vision by Zechariah (5:1-4), occupies an important place in the first summons of Ezekiel (Ezek. 2:9-10).

While the voice and posture of prophecy appear clearly enough in Zechariah, it is equally true that Zechariah, along with Haggai, is allowing prophecy to yield its place to priesthood. This tendency is all the more pronounced when we compare Zechariah with Third Isaiah, who also preached some time after the first return from exile (Isa. 56–66). In the latter the independent voice of prophecy in favor of foreigners (Isa. 56) and against abuses in sanctuary worship from unworthy priests (Isa. 57–59) rings out much more stridently. While Third Isaiah is one of the final representatives of northern prophecy in a line of succession with Hosea, Jeremiah, and Second Isaiah (Isa. 40–55), Zechariah's pedigree is to be traced more emphatically to southern prophets, especially Ezekiel, who center the postexilic revival of the people upon the Jerusalem temple.

THE HISTORICAL BACKGROUND FOR ZECHARIAH

The setting for Zechariah's career as a prophet is the same as that for Haggai. Darius has overcome the revolts around the empire at the time of his seizure of the throne. The memory of this shaking of the heavens and of the earth remains vivid with Haggai (Hag. 2:6, 21) and with Zechariah (Zech. 1:11). Yet with Zechariah we sense that the high expectations of Haggai for a quick messianic fulfillment did not materialize. Zechariah must settle for a long-term messianism and so attends more carefully to the necessary steps of purifying the temple and the priesthood. His occasional, favorable outlook towards foreigners (2:11; 8:22-23) may be prompted by the help given by Darius for rebuilding the temple and for permitting free passage from Babylon back to the promised land.

It is possible, according to Théophane Chary (*Aggée—Zacharie Malachie*, 37), that Zechariah was prompted to speak by the arrival of a fresh contingent of Jewish immigrants from Babylon (cf. 6:10; 7:2), or else he was following an impulse of excitement from Haggai's preaching.

While Haggai's sermons, at least as recorded and dated in his book, extended only from 29 August to 18 December 520 B.C., Zechariah began preaching 27 October 520 and his last sermon is placed on 7 December 518—according to the system for interpreting the lunar calendar and years of Darius' reign worked out by Joyce G. Baldwin (*Haggai, Zechariah, Malachi*, 29).

For the conditions in the land of Judah at this time, see the Introduction to Haggai.

THE BOOK OF ZECHARIAH

The eight chapters of Zechariah consist of:

1:1-6	Introduction
1:7–6:15	Eight Visions (see below, 61, for further divisions)
7:1–8:23	Sermon about Fasting; Messianic Promises

Within this overall plan we detect the work of the editor in many places. In the long introduction to Zechariah's visions and preaching (1:1-6) the editor carefully associates Zechariah with the prophetic tradition of Israel, referring twice to the former prophets and incorporating strong motifs from Jeremiah about returning to the Lord and turning from evil ways (cf. Jer. 3:22; 4:1; 15:19). By using the Babylonian name of the month in Zech. 1:7 and 7:1 it is possible that the editor is associating the events in Israel with world history, or more correctly that world history eventually receives its true meaning in relation to Israel!

The editor remains ambivalent towards Zerubbabel and the Davidic dynasty. As noted, he sometimes deliberately inserts lines about the exclusive role of Zerubbabel. He seems to highlight the Davidic heir, first in a section that deals as well with the high priest Joshua (cf. 4:6-10 within 4:1-14) and second in a narrative about Joshua alone (cf. 6:12-13 within 6:9-15). When, on the contrary, the editor uses the title *king* with Darius (7:1), he may be inferring that royalty has passed from David's family and that Israel must think only of a foreign world monarch. This position will become particularly true with the disappearance of Zerubbabel. This abrupt ending of the Davidic dynasty may be due to Persian intervention sometime before the editor compiled this book.

The editor forms an "inclusion," repeating at the end in chs. 7–8 key words or ideas from the beginning in ch. 1. The former prophets are mentioned in 1:4-6 and in 7:7, and the nations are referred to in a favorable way in 1:15 and in 8:22-23. Inclusion is used not just to round out the entire work but also to show the consistency and interaction of all the sections in the one plan of God. Inclusion can also be employed in reverse. While both the earth and nations are said to be "at rest" in 1:11, 15, the intense activity in and towards Jerusalem by Gentiles and diaspora Jews at the end (8:20-23) stirs with great possibilities for the future. By reversing an idea the editor indicates to us that the work of the prophet must continue. The end or "rest" is not yet in sight. We will return to this idea in speaking of eschatology in the next section.

THE MESSAGE OF ZECHARIAH

1. *A Transcendent God.* As is typical in most postexilic literature, Yahweh becomes ever more distant and supreme. There is "a spiritualization of the notion of God" (Théophane Chary, *Aggée—Zacharie Malachie,* 47). God no longer speaks directly to the prophet. As seen in the inaugural visions of Isaiah (Isa. 6) and Ezekiel (Ezek. 1–3), Yahweh is surrounded with resplendent glory, but in Zechariah Yahweh is not seen in any way at all. Yahweh is always intensely present but beyond sight and hearing. As a result, angels become ever more important as go-betweens and interpreters.

If Yahweh speaks directly, the statements occur in sections that seem like addenda to the vision (Zech. 2:6-12) or to the preaching (ch. 8). Again we mark an ambiguity in Zechariah's intentions, or perhaps we are detecting a stage along the way towards an ever more elusive and transcendent sense of deity.

The prophet's stance before Yahweh is summed up very well in a statement at the end of ch. 2. The inspiration for it came from earlier, preexilic prophecy, in this case from Hab. 2:20, but the incorporation within an account of dreams or visions is typical of Zechariah. This postexilic prophet is quite different from Habakkuk, who even argues with God and questions God. Zechariah's narrative is leading up to a vision about Joshua the high priest standing humbly, even sinfully, before God in the heavenly sanctuary. In no way whatsoever is the high priest in a posture to question or challenge God. He is to be cleansed and forgiven by God. Immediately before this episode Zechariah called for humble adoration:

> Be silent, all flesh, before the LORD; for he has roused himself from his holy dwelling. (Zech. 2:13)

2. *Social Justice.* Other theological features have already been discussed, like the emergence of the high priest and the importance of

the temple liturgy. This impression is reenforced from the primacy given to purity not only for the people and the high priest (ch. 3) but also for the land (5:5-11). Nonetheless, we still find the prophetical insistence upon social justice (5:1-5). This latter point becomes all the more emphatic in the sermon recorded in ch. 7, which one writer called "one of the finest summaries of the teaching of the former prophets" (Ralph L. Smith, *Micah—Malachi*, 225).

3. *Messianic Age.* For Haggai the promised moment of fulfillment occurred with the rebuilding of the temple. He recognized this episode as shaking the heavens and the earth and the nations. The finale will come "in a little while" (Hag. 2:6). Zechariah, by contrast, slows down the process! He shows himself to be much more conscious than Haggai of the need of purification, and he steps away from Haggai in his insistence upon social justice. More realistic, Zechariah settles for a long-term messianism. If this is the case, then we need to be cautious about attaching the term of eschatology to the preaching and visions of Zechariah. He is certainly closer to the finale or end, as the Greek word behind eschatology means, than preexilic prophets, but similar to them he recognizes the need first of much foundational work on justice, sincerity, and purity.

Another obstacle to the final fulfillment of Israel's promises comes from a new phenomenon in the postexilic age. More Jews were now living outside of the promised land than inside it. Their continuous presence among foreign peoples raised more acutely the question of the latter's relationship to Israel and the Covenant. There is little or no problem of accepting the genuine religious quality about Jews living in the Diaspora. They are called to come on pilgrimage to the holy city (Zech. 2:10-13; 8:23). Zechariah's attitude towards the Gentiles, however, again turns out to be ambivalent. At times they are invited to come to Jerusalem (2:8, 13; 8:23), but at other times their land is the dumping ground of Israel's sins (5:5-11). The nations are even the object of the Lord's anger (1:15). Such ambivalence towards the nations and uncertainty about the end are not characteristic of literature that is properly eschatological (e.g., Isa. 24–27).

In any case, Zechariah's view is exclusively centripetal as diaspora Jews and at times the Gentiles are invited to come to Jerusalem; there is no centrifugal movement outward to them nor an acceptance of them in their own homeland and culture.

The final chapters of Zechariah, chs. 9–14, became a rich mine for NT writers. We reserve for the Introduction to chs. 9–14 the treatment of NT messianic interpretation.

MY WORDS OVERTAKE YOU
Zechariah 1:1-6

SPEAKING WITH THE PROPHETIC MANTLE

The editor is introducing the eight visions within chs. 1–6, and in doing so links Zechariah closely with Israel's prophetic tradition. The superscription in 1:1 with date and the prophet's name follows the pattern already seen in Haggai and eleven times earlier in Ezekiel (Hag. 1:1, 15; 2:1, 10, 20; Ezek. 1:2-3; 8:1; 20:1, etc.). "The eighth month, in the second year of Darius" began on 27 October 520 (Joyce G. Baldwin, *Haggai, Zechariah, Malachi*, 87); Zechariah started preaching two months after the beginning of Haggai's ministry.

Zechariah's sermon follows this pattern: the anger of the Lord (v. 2), a call for repentance (vv. 3-6a), and the resultant conversion (v. 6b). The language is wooden and repetitive: e.g., in v. 3 recurring stereotyped formulas take more space than the message itself! The word "return" reminds us of preaching by Jeremiah (cf. Jer. 3:22; 4:1; 15:19), while the added reference to "your fathers" recalls 2 Chr. 30:6-9. A phrase from Zech. 1:3 is quoted in Mal. 3:7. Not only a prophetic tradition but even a prophetic vocabulary is being established. Zechariah, moreover, is extending his background beyond that of Haggai to be more inclusive of traditions from the former northern kingdom represented by Jeremiah.

The editor is consciously linking Zechariah with what is now an accepted corpus of prophetical literature, here called "the former prophets," referring particularly to such major figures as Jeremiah and Ezekiel. (Today in Jewish tradition the phrase refers to a specific section of the Hebrew Bible, namely the books of Joshua, Judges, Samuel, and Kings, while the books of the three major and twelve minor prophets are called the "Latter Prophets.") The Latter, or classical, prophets with books to their name tended not to call themselves "prophets" until the time of Ezekiel; the first of them, Amos, even rejected the title (Amos 7:14). It was the later editors of the preaching and writing of these extraordinary persons who attached the title prophet, generally in the introductions or superscriptions to their work. With Zechariah, however, we are entering the age of the Bible as a collection of accepted inspired books, to be quoted and to be applied as a norm for living. To refer to Zechariah as a prophet in the same context of quoting the "former prophets," places their mantle upon Zechariah and assures Israel that the prophetical age continues.

Several times in this short sermon Zechariah declares that prophecy has been fulfilled in the destruction of the homeland and in the Exile, yet this negative side was not meant for Israel's extermination but for Israel's purification as a humble, obedient, faith-filled people. Such a statement is indeed reassuring, but it also leaves us with a theological difficulty. It is reassuring to know that every event is within the wise and directive hand of God, a point argued repeatedly by Second Isaiah during the Exile (cf. Isa. 41:21-29; 43:9-12; ch. 48). The Exile was not due to Yahweh's powerlessness nor to the Lord's infidelity to the promises pledged to Israel in the Covenant (Samuel Amsler, *Aggée, Zacharie 1-8,* 56). Nonetheless, we are plagued with this difficulty: How can God turn against Israel in such a horrendously cruel way, with military invasion, destruction of the homeland, and exile in a foreign country, whatever be the noble, divine purpose in punishing Israel for sin? Earlier, the prophet Habakkuk put the same question to God and in reply was given no explanation, only a call to further confidence in Yahweh:

> If [the vision or explanation] seem slow, wait for it; . . . the righteous shall live by his faith. (Hab. 2:3-4)

Similarly, Zechariah does not explain but simply reaffirms the ancient faith of Israel.

Twice in Zech. 1:2 the Hebrew word for "angry" is attributed to Yahweh. It is found to be the Lord's reaction against Israel not only in earlier traditions, such as Deut. 1:34; 9:19, but especially during and after the Exile, frequently in cultic lamentation (Isa. 47:6; 54:9; 57:16-17; 64:5, 9; Lam. 5:22). As S. Paul Re'emi comments on the song of lament in Lam. 5:22, "The worshipper is far from counting on cheap grace [and the] conscience is tortured by doubt: 'Or hast thou utterly rejected us? Art thou exceedingly angry with us?'" (*God's People in Crisis,* 132).

By means of this link with the traditions of covenant and prophecy Israel not only survives the ordeal of the Exile but also recognizes the hidden but real presence of the Lord within it. This reference to the Lord's anger occurs, however, in a fragmentary verse (Zech.

1:2), loosely attached to the context here (cf. Petersen, 129). It does interrupt the flow from v. 1 to v. 3. As is often enough the case, our finest insights take us by surprise and at first hardly fit into the context of our normal thinking. The most insightful moments of prophecy belong to the pure of heart who alone can rightfully ascend the mount of the Lord and for a moment at least glimpse the mystifying presence of God in most unlikely times or circumstances (cf. 1 Kgs. 19:4-18; Jer. 23:18-22).

Prophecy was not spoken from a philosophical podium but from an instinct of faith in Israel's purest ideals and God's total commitment to the Covenant. Prophecy, consequently, reaffirmed the basic morality of the Decalogue (Deut. 5:6-21), but also envisaged it in the context of the Lord's covenant love (cf. Hos. 2:19-23; 4:1-2; Jer. 31:31-37). Zechariah states it as simply as possible in 1:6, following the language of Deuteronomy: "my words and my statutes, which I commanded my servants the prophets" (cf. Deut. 4:5; 6:1). Prophecy, as stated in the Introduction to this book, found its continuity through close collaboration with Israel's central, organizational line in the Torah and its application by priests and civil rulers. And so it happened that "my words and my statutes . . . did . . . overtake [you and] your fathers." While prophets died, as Zech. 1:5 admits, their words did not, through the permanence bestowed upon them through priesthood and torah.

GOD'S INITIATIVE IN REPENTANCE

The prophetical imperative, "return to me, says the LORD of hosts, and I will return to you, says the LORD of hosts" (v. 3), seems to condition our return to grace upon our own human initiative. Yet at once this position is challenged by the thrice repeated formula, "thus says the LORD of hosts," as though we never would have thought of it, had the Lord not drummed the idea into us! We are reminded of the penitent woman in Luke 7:36-50, whose return to grace, Jesus declared, was due to her love: "her sins, which are many, are forgiven, for she loved much." Yet the bold initiative of the sinful woman, entering an august and forbidding assembly of law-abiding people, meant that she had been observing the kind and compassionate Jesus and may have even heard him say: "I have not come to call the righteous, but sinners to repentance" (Luke 5:32).

The strong love of God, attracting us to a new confidence in divine compassion and forgiveness, appears magnificently in what is the centerpiece of the book of Exodus, chs. 32–34. Exodus is probably Israel's most important book of covenant and law, and at its center these three chapters provide an exceptional method for interpreting law. We first observe Moses' shattering the tablets of the law at the sight of Israel's idolatry (ch. 32), then his intense desire to see the face of the Lord in all its glory (ch. 33), and finally the awesome moment, when Moses stood atop Mount Sinai with a new set of tablets in his arms and heard the Lord passing by and declaring:

> The Lord, the LORD, a God merciful and gracious, slow to anger, and abounding in steadfast love and faithfulness, keeping steadfast love for thousands, forgiving iniquity and transgression and sin, but who will by no means clear the guilty, visiting the iniquity of the fathers . . . to the third and the fourth generation. (Exod. 34:6-7)

Such blinding glory thereafter emanated from Moses' face that he had to wear a veil over it except when conversing with God (Exod. 34:29-35).

Law is to be interpreted from the setting of the Lord's "steadfast love and faithfulness . . . for thousands [of generations]," and in this way does it lead to a mystic union with God. This contemplative wonder of faith and this loving bond with God must subsist within liturgy, otherwise liturgy will degenerate into idolatry. This vision of God's luminous compassion "will by no means clear the guilty." Sin is rightly understood as an evil act that brings its own fallout of sorrow and guilt. Unless sin is called by its right name, forgiveness and compassion become meaningless. Yet punishment, extending "to the third and the fourth generation," is surpassed by compassion "for thousands [of generations]." It is the faith-perception of such a God, already suffused within Israel, which first beckons towards repentance and anticipates any initiative on our part to return to the Lord. God's anger towards the sinful is swallowed up within God's compassion for the repentant sinner.

THE EIGHT VISIONS
Zechariah 1:7–6:8

DREAMS AND VISIONS FOR DIVINE COMMUNICATION

Several questions can be raised about visions in the Bible—with serious implications for a theological commentary. Are these accounts referring to: (1) dreams, *supernaturally granted by God,* so that in moments of ecstasy a person is granted to see what is otherwise invisible because of distance in space or time? or (2) a *literary style,* in which the speaker or writer draws upon memories and experiences, either sacred or nonreligious, ancient traditions and stories, mythologies and folklore, and then casts the message in the literary form of a dream, in order to inculcate the mysterious, even unearthly aspect of the message? or (3) a *combination of both,* a dream or vision from God as a way of God's communicating with the prophet, and secondly a literary style by which the prophet is able to communicate the message adequately to others.

Some visions are so highly stylized in their literary form (e.g., Amos 7:1-9; 8:1-2) that in their case we are inclined to the second (2) explanation above. Still other narratives of visions carefully follow a standard literary form, like the "call narrative" of prophets (e.g., Isa. 6; 40:1-8; Ezek. 1–3), yet each with significant differences in literary style and distinctive religious influences on the prophets, that at least the third (3) position seems convincing. In any case, we can never rule out the more common understanding of divinely induced dreams according to the first (1) explanation above. Dreams, however, are recorded in the Bible, not simply for the sake of the dreamer but for imparting a message to Israel, and therefore some type of accepted literary form of "dream narrative" is almost always employed by the writer or speaker.

One of the most common names for a prophet is *seer* or *visionary*—in Hebrew, *ro'eh* or *hozeh,* "one who sees [with unique insight]," sometimes used in a complimentary way as in 1 Sam. 9:9-11, or with sarcasm and condemnation as in Isa. 29:9-10 and Mic.

58

3:5-8. A dreamer is an easy victim to manipulation or hallucination, or at least to excessive optimism.

We can be assured, through our faith in the book of Zechariah as God's inspired word, that the prophet experienced a mighty impact of the Lord's presence, possibly in the shape of a vision, and that the final form of the book was directed by the Lord to communicate an inspired revelation from God, important for his own time and valid for all ages. We cannot be as certain about the human or natural steps used for the formulation of the message by the original visionary/writer, nor about the stages of editorial work before the message reached its present form in the Bible. The final shape of the message is God's inspired word for us; everyone responsible for various steps along the way shared in the inspiration of the original prophet. Concerning the many steps leading up to the present form of the book or account in our Bible, God makes use of any worthy human style of reasoning and communication, whether the communication be from God to the inspired author or from the latter to the people Israel. Dreams are a normal, worthy form of receiving information. And to speak *as though* one had a dream inspired by God, as did Martin Luther King, Jr., in one of his most famous discourses ("I have a dream . . ."), is also normal, worthy, and very often extremely effective in communicating a message that one is convinced to be from God.

Various elements contribute to the narrative of Zechariah's visions. Some are mythological and are drawn from the preexisting Canaanite religion, others are liturgical features from Israel's temple and sanctuary worship, still others are literary details from earlier biblical accounts. David L. Petersen contends that in the visions Zechariah was speaking from within the context of normative Israelite religious traditions ("Zechariah's Visions: A Theological Perspective," *VT* 34 [1984]: 195-206). Petersen also points out in his commentary (*Haggai and Zechariah 1–8*, 144-45) that other details, such as horsemen patrolling the roads, were images readily available from the Persian system of security along the main arteries of the empire. Théophane Chary (*Aggée—Zacharie Malachie*, 57-117) has discussed effectively the mythological features in the symbolism of Zechariah. Further, more general background is provided by Othmar Keel, *The Symbolism of the Biblical World*, 56-60, enabling us to recognize a hidden symbolical or metaphorical meaning in such details as mountains, colors, springs of water, and depths of the earth. Still other items have biblical precedent, like a divine council, where angels or spirits are present before Yahweh, ready to accomplish the divine will (1 Kgs. 22:19-23; Job 1–2). The material of Zechariah's dreams, therefore, come from a variety of sources.

A literary pattern is perceptible within the eight visions of Zechariah. Visions I-III and V-VIII proceed with an introduction, a description of what is seen, a question from the prophet about its meaning, and the explanation from the accompanying angel. As we shall see, editorial additions or modifications occur, and vision IV is completely on its own! The presence of an angel to guide and interpret was already present in the final visions of Ezekiel (Ezek. 40:3) and will become ever more prominent as prophetic literature continues to evolve into its still more visionary, more symbolic, more transcendent form with such apocalyptic books as Daniel (Dan. 7:16; 8:16; cf. Rev. 17:1; 21:9).

The editor introduced all eight visions with a single date at Zech. 1:7. It is possible that all took place within a span of twenty-four hours. What is more important for us, however, is the editor's desire to unify all the visions, to balance each one with the others, and—like the editing of Haggai's preaching (by the same person?)—to expand with a wider worldview whatever may have been the prophet's narrowness and to adapt it to the fast-changing political situation. Joyce G. Baldwin (*Haggai, Zechariah, Malachi,* 80, 93) points out a chiastic arrangement of the visions: the first vision corresponding with the last or eighth through the presence of horses and chariots; the two center visions, the fourth and the fifth, each focusing upon designated leaders. Whether or not the second and third visions, as Baldwin suggests, parallel the sixth and seventh in the themes of threats against Israel and the cleansing of sin from the land remains problematical.

If the visions center around the temple and its ceremonies, especially the dedication of the new temple that is central in the mission and theology of Haggai and Zechariah, then the following double sequence can be recognized. The first series on the left below prepares for the temple foundation, the second series on the right insists upon the purity and justice of God's people. The historical role of Zerubbabel in the prophetic discourse of 3:8-10 + 4:6b-10a supports both series and so is recognized as central and foundational.

(1) 1:7-17
     Vision of the
     Four Horsemen

    (2) 1:18-21
        vision of four horns
        nations cast down

        (3) 2:1-13
            vision of new
            Jerusalem

            (4) 3:1-10
                High Priest purified
                and exalted

            (5) 4:1-14
                Vision of Two Anointed Ones,
                High priest and prince

(8) 6:1-8
     Four Chariots

(7) 5:5-11
     Vision of ephah
     evil removed

(6) 5:1-4
     Vision of scroll;
     evil removed from
     Jerusalem

It is helpful to point out the different enumeration of verses in chs. 1–2:

Hebrew; Greek; *NAB*		Latin Vulgate; *RSV*
1:1-17	=	1:1-17
2:1-4	=	1:18-21
2:5-16	=	2:1-13
3:1ff.	=	3:1ff.

VISION I: A DISAPPOINTING PEACE AND A NEW HOPE

Zechariah 1:7-17

VISION OF THE FOUR HORSEMEN

After the initial superscription, intended for all eight visions (1:7), the section consists principally of the vision of the four horsemen who patrol the earth (vv. 8-15) and secondarily of a new oracle of hope (vv. 16-17). Horses were the "engines of war," donkeys the carriers of peace (cf. 9:9). Horses are frequently introduced into the visions or discourses of Zechariah, especially in the latter part of the prophecy (9:10; 10:3, 5; 12:4; 14:15, 20), where the tone becomes ever more militant. *Four* horsemen indicates a patrol for all four corners of the earth. The symbolism of the horses' colors does not seem to enter into the prophecy.

Following the chronology of Joyce G. Baldwin (*Haggai, Zechariah, Malachi,* 29, 94), we locate the twenty-fourth day of the eleventh month on 15 February 519 B.C., two months after Haggai's final oracle (Hag. 2:10, 20), three months after Zechariah's first intervention (Zech. 1:1). As is more evident from the Hebrew text, the phrase "which is the month of Shebat" is clearly a gloss or explanatory addition, influenced by the Chronicler who edited the material in Ezra, Nehemiah, and 1-2 Chronicles. Only in the two books of Chronicles, as well as in Zech. 1:7 and 7:1, do we find the Babylonian names of months. Otherwise numbers are used for successive months of the year. While a detail such as this seems inconsequential to modern readers, it gives an insight, as David L. Petersen indicates (*Haggai and Zechariah 1-8,* 138), into the attitude of the editor, intent not only to locate Israel's religious history within world history, but also to show that eventually Israel's history will surpass the longevity and boundaries even of the Persian Empire.

The final words in 1:7, "and Zechariah said," read differently in the Hebrew, which refers to the Lord as the speaker. As a matter of fact, no words are spoken in the following v. 8, but the Lord grants a vision to the prophet. As at other times with prophecy, the vision or the dramatic action constitutes a message, sometimes beyond the power of human words adequately to explain (cf. Ezek. 1–3), or if words are used, by themselves they will not make sense without the account of the vision or symbolic action. In Ezek. 5:1-5, for instance, the words "This is Jerusalem" say nothing specific about Jerusalem; they need to be associated with Ezekiel's somewhat weird symbolic action with hair cut from his head; and the action is all the more weird and meaningless without the words. Words and actions together, however, constitute an unmistakable and powerful prophecy about the impending destruction of Jerusalem.

A number of details heighten the mysterious or ecstatic nature of Zechariah's first vision. In Zech. 1:8, "I saw in the night" reads more directly in the Hebrew, "I saw this night," like staring into darkness and gradually perceiving a mysterious object that turns into a vision. Within a number of psalms, prayer through the night brought the worshipper into close, contemplative union with the Lord (Ps. 8:3; 42:3; 119:147-148). Into this darkness someone appears to the prophet: "And behold, a man." This individual is the first of several heavenly visitors and shows up again in Zech. 1:10; *an angel* is present in vv. 9, 12, and 14. We find that v. 11 is spoken by the other horsemen, declaring that "we have patrolled the earth, and behold, all the earth remains at rest." Although v. 13 states that "the LORD answered gracious and comforting words to the angel," the exact message is not recorded and the overall impression is bewildering.

While Zechariah's vision does not place him within the august chambers of the heavenly council, as happened to Micaiah (1 Kgs. 22:19-23) as well as to First and Second Isaiah (Isa. 6, 40), the vision does locate Zechariah in a sacred area as is indicated, among other details, by the mention of "myrtle." This plant is associated with the mysterious presence of God within great moments of Israel's history (Isa. 41:19; 55:13) or within great liturgical feasts (Neh. 8:15).

The Hebrew words in Zech. 1:11, "all the earth remains at rest," can imply a rest that is evil and undesirable (Isa. 30:7; Jer. 48:11) or a rest free of military action and therefore good (Isa. 30:15-18). The latter, as Petersen indicates (145-46), is especially the case during the Exile and afterwards (Isa. 14:7; Jer. 47:6-7; Ezek. 16:42). Zechariah is probably referring to the end of civil war, once Darius had overcome all opposition to his seizure of the throne in 522. (See the Introduction to this volume.) "The shaking of the heavens and of the earth," however, by the impact of these revolts upon the Persian Empire did not bring splendor and treasures to the Jerusalem temple, and so the hopes of the prophet Haggai were left unfulfilled

(Hag. 2:6-9). As Jeremiah had pointed out before the Exile, prophecies of peace and prosperity require more careful scrutiny (Jer. 28:7-9). Yet the eventual spread of peace, while not measuring up to the grandeur of Haggai, was nonetheless beneficial to Israel.

The phrase in Zech. 1:12: "seventy years," brings to mind other memories from the preaching of Jeremiah (Jer. 25:11, spoken in 605; Jer. 29:10, spoken in 593). "Seventy years," for all its symbolism, carried a stern message from Jeremiah that the Exile would last its full course, but also a consoling assurance that it would certainly end. Edward Lipiński, in studying the Black Stone of the Assyrian emperor Esarhaddon (681-669), definitely shows that the number seventy was used *symbolically* about a time of divine anger ("Recherches sur le livre de Zacharie," *VT* 20 [1970]: 38). However, if we tabulate from the beginning of Babylon's plans for the first seige of Jerusalem (590/589; 2 Kgs. 24:10) to the time of this vision (520), the seventy years show up in a remarkably accurate way!

The message from the returning angels after patrolling the earth blend Yahweh's anger and tender concern for Israel in Zech. 1:14-16,

> Thus says the Lord of hosts: I am exceedingly jealous for Jerusalem. . . . I am very angry with the nations that are at ease; for while I was angry but a little they furthered the disaster. . . . I have returned to Jerusalem with compassion; my house shall be built in it. . . .

The Hebrew word "jealous" may be connected with a similar Arabic word for dyeing an object black or red; metaphorically it indicates the visible appearance of strong interior emotions (Baldwin, 101-2). In the Bible it is associated with Yahweh's personal commitment to the Covenant with Israel (Exod. 20:5; 34:14) and with the Lord's anger either at Israel for drifting away from the Covenant or at the nations for interfering with the Lord's covenantal plans for Israel (Ezek. 16:38, 42).

When the text refers to "the nations that are at ease," they are being censured for their proud satisfaction with themselves, even though they have passed beyond the bounds of what Yahweh intended in punishing Israel through the Exile (Isa. 10:15; 40:1-2; 47:5-17).

The account of the vision concludes with a new oracle in Zech. 1:16-17. It speaks positively for Israel, drawing images from Isa. 40 and Ezek. 40–48 and extending the Lord's blessings from the temple outward upon the city Jerusalem and still farther to the cities of Judah. This is an image that will be picked up again, in a still more grandiose way, at the end of the prophecy of Zechariah in 13:1 and 14:16-18. In 1:17 the adverb "again" is repeated three times to re-enforce the Lord's intention to bring "prosperity," "comfort," and divine election to Jerusalem. This final verse turns the first vision with its message from the four horsemen into a glorious paean of prophetical and liturgical traditions.

ISRAEL'S ELECTION; THE NATIONS' NON-ELECTION

The first vision, granted that it originally ended at v. 15, would have stopped without a conclusion! The Lord's deeply interior and "jealous" love for Israel was reaffirmed; the Lord's anger at the nations was clearly stated. Yet the nations were resting in their conquests that had gone beyond the Lord's purpose for Israel. First Isaiah clearly stated this haughty interference by the nations (Isa. 10:15), and Second Isaiah implied it by stating that Israel "has received from the LORD's hands double [i.e., more than the Lord intended] for all her sins" (Isa. 40:2c).

As Friedrich Huber has shown in his book, *Jahwe, Juda und die anderen Völker beim Propheten Jesaja,* the prophets enabled Israel to take a serious step forward in accepting the nations in the drama of salvation. The nations are not simply, as in the theology of the books of Joshua and Judges, the Lord's instrument for punishing a sinful and therefore weakened Israel. Military invasion and even the Exile became important features not just for punishing but also for purifying Israel, so that the "darkness" and "woe" that they brought upon Israel were the Lord's "creation" (cf. Isa. 45:7, where the strictly theological word for creation, Hebrew *bara',* twice refers to darkness and woe). The nations were being viewed *positively* as the Lord's agents in the renewal of Israel.

So important was the Exile for prophets like Haggai and Zechariah, that only those Israelites (and their descendants) who were taken into Babylon and then returned from this foreign country were the true remnant, the authentic Israel, against the claims of the "people of the land" who were left behind first by the Assyrians and later by the Babylonians. This point was discussed in the Introduction and in the commentary on Haggai (see Hag. 2:10-14).

Even though here the outlook of Zechariah is negative towards the nations, nonetheless the prophet reenforced the care with which Yahweh will make use of them. They can go so far, and no further, without risking the Lord's anger. Their response to Israel had its well defined limits.

Zechariah's understanding of this theological role of the nations leads to other observations, seemingly criss-crossing in contrary directions. Clearly enough, if the first vision ended at Zech. 1:15, Zechariah was unhappy with the results of the nations' activity towards Israel, yet he was willing to let the case rest at this point. He was not, therefore, a political activist, urging revolt and a military response. The nonpolitical, perhaps pacifist attitude becomes clearer when we reread the editorial addition to the first vision in vv. 16-17. It is up to Yahweh to extend "the measuring line . . . over Jerusalem" (something that can insinuate restoration; cf. Jer. 31:38-39; Ezek. 47:3). Jerusalem's prosperity, moreover, depends, as with the prophet Haggai, principally upon the rebuilding of the temple. This focusing upon the temple is all the more impressive with Zechariah's fearful and unhappy attention to the nations. He could have first demanded, for Judah's security, the rebuilding of the city walls, something that did not happen till the arrival of Nehemiah some eighty years later (cf. Neh. 1–6).

Yet, this otherworldly, nonpolitical attitude of Zechariah in rebuilding the temple before the city walls is combined with a careful watch over international politics and events. Yahweh was continuing, ever since the days of Abraham and Moses, to achieve Israel's redemption in the world's political setting. Israel did not emerge initially as a political reality with its own unique history, but rather Israel was a conglomerate of many races and cultures at its origin (cf. Exod. 12:38; Num 11:4). Implied in this historical setting is the delicate, but significant theological position: neither race nor nationality nor prestige was essential for a true Israelite, only a humble attitude towards the Lord the Redeemer (cf. Deut. 7:7-8; Ezek. 16:3). Non-Israelites are certainly capable of responding to grace and election by Yahweh, similar to that granted to Israel. Zechariah does not draw such a conclusion (Amos 9:7 seems to take that step), but the implication is present.

If Israel and especially Jerusalem are the object of the Lord's special election, this elect status of Israel, setting the people off from the nonelect nations, holds within itself, secretly and mysteriously, a call to the nations sooner or later to join this election.

VISION II: THE NATIONS ARE CAST DOWN

Zechariah 1:18-21

BEHOLD, FOUR HORNS!

This new vision is reported in a style typical of other parts of Zechariah and of the Bible. (1) A vision is announced in a way that recognizes human freedom, "I lifted my eyes," but emphasizes the divine wonder, granted beyond the scope of human ingenuity: "I looked, and behold! [there were] . . . !" The Hebrew word, "I looked," implies that the prophet is already acting as a "seer." (2) The description of the vision is presented quickly and vaguely, "four horns." (3) A question from the seer, "What are these?" extends a baffling aura over the scope of the vision. (4) An explanation from a heavenly messenger implies a communication beyond human wisdom.

Stylistically this short account is held together by the repetition of key words: to *scatter* in the lands of exile (vv. 19 and 21); and to *lift up* one's eyes obediently (v. 18); to fail to *lift up* one's head because of defeat (v. 21a); or to *lift up* one's horn defiantly (v. 21b).

This brief account about the destruction of the nations complements the first and third visions. In these latter places the nations are left unpunished after pillaging and scattering Israel. Whatever openness towards foreigners is seen in the first and third visions is here closed off. This text may be reflecting not just a strong bias against the nations but possibly a liturgical rule, roundly excluding the nations from participation in the restored temple. The OT, as we saw in the preceding section, has no clear, systematized theology about the salvation of the nations.

The nations are symbolized by four horns. By this late period of Zechariah the Hebrew word for "horns" has gathered a long and rich tradition. Originally it referred to the horns of powerful animals and quickly became a symbol of strength and virility. To lift up horns signified victory (1 Sam. 2:1, literally, "my horn is exalted") or arrogance (Ps. 75:5-6); to lower horns implies defeat (Job 16:15, literally, "I have laid my horn in the dust"). "Horn" becomes a title for God, who is acclaimed for strength (2 Sam. 22:3, "the horn of my salvation"). Because the altar symbolized divine presence, it is not surprising that the altar was decorated with horns on all four corners (Exod. 27:2) and to grasp them is to rely on God for protection (1 Kgs. 1:50). Rams' horns summoned the people to worship and announced great festivals (Ps. 81:3). The symbol has become so rich that the type of animal which supplies the horns becomes unimportant.

The numeral four includes the four corners of the altar (Baruch Halpern, "The Ritual Background of Zechariah's Temple Song," *CBQ* 40{1978]: 177-78), but it probably reaches out to include all forces hostile to Israel. It is all-embracing like the four horsemen in the first vision and the four chariots in the last. That same inclusiveness is seen in the reference to "Judah, Israel, and Jerusalem," destroyed by foreigners; the northern kingdom of Israel and the southern kingdom of Judah are again reunited at Jerusalem in God's plans for restoration.

Restoration comes through the action of the "four smiths." This Hebrew word is very generic of an artisan who works with wood (2 Sam. 5:11), metal (1 Sam 13:19), or stone (Exod. 28:11). The smiths are "coming" and are now in the process of destroying the four horns. God can never be passively present!

A RELIGIOUS CONQUEST OF WORLD EVIL

The restoration of the temple may have seemed insignificant to the Persians; it was happening in many places of their empire according to their benevolent policy of allowing people exiled by the Assyrians and Babylonians to return to their homelands and reconstruct their houses of worship. Zechariah views the event as the center of world history and the temple itself as the capital of the world. All empires will sooner or later pay homage to the Lord who is enthroned at the Jerusalem temple. In this vision the homage is expressed by military defeat of the nations and their own scattering into exile.

Haggai had a similar idea, expressing it in terms of the shaking of "the heavens and the earth and the sea and the dry land" (Hag. 2:6), and it was remarked at that time that his language was most probably influenced by the revolts across the Persian Empire when Darius seized the throne. In composing this vision Zechariah may have been similarly influenced by world politics.

Theologically, both prophets are visionaries who do not deny political and military reality but see a divine force within it. Through human events God is reaching towards a goal beyond human comprehension, perceived only in vision.

Today the Church and its mission cannot escape the reality of our day. In fact, it must interact vigorously, yet not from a political or military base but rather from a conviction that wholesome morality in obedience to God will win the day and lead to a bonding of faithful people in the new Jerusalem. No one will be lost, no matter how far away they have been scattered; oppressors will be cast down, no matter how brutal and uncontrollable their power. They will be undone by their own unrestrained greed and reckless use of strength. Here is how the Bible interprets the *lex talionis* of an "eye for eye, tooth for tooth" (Exod. 21:24).

If this vision is short and abrupt, there are times of great sorrow and world tension when we do not have the luxury of time to philosophize. We are sustained only by the interior conviction: God, all powerful like four smiths, shatters and demolishes the diabolical "four" horns of evil across the universe.

VISION III:
THE NEW JERUSALEM
Zechariah 2:1-13

SING AND REJOICE, O DAUGHTER OF ZION

After the vision of the new Jerusalem in vv. 1-5 (for literary form see the introductory remarks with 1:18-21), prophetic oracles offer some explanation, first in vv. 6-9 by calling upon the people to "flee from the land of the north"—that is, from Babylon—because of Israel's experience of mistreatment from gentile nations, then in vv. 10-12 calling for joy over God's hopes for the new homeland. The oracle concludes with a liturgical invocation for silence in v. 13.

Stylistically, according to the Hebrew text, the prose in vv. 1-5 modulates into poetic lines in vv. 6-13. These latter are divided into two stanzas, as Joyce Baldwin points out (*Haggai, Zechariah, Malachi,* 107), each beginning with a double imperative and continuing with a divine message and the prophet's comments. The final verse leaves us in silent awe before the Lord, who is roused to a new mighty presence with the people.

The *measuring line* in vv. 1-2 does not reflect Amos 7:7-9 with its vision of a measuring line that marks off an area for destruction, but rather the sign of hope in Ezek. 40:3; 41:13 about the new, spacious temple. In Zechariah's vision, moreover, the sacred boundaries reach beyond the temple to include not only the reconstructed holy city of Jerusalem, but also the "breadth and . . . length" of the expansive living quarters of numberless people in a city without walls.

Two angels appear in Zech. 2:3, almost as though the second one is sent to correct any misunderstanding in the mind of the first about the new Jerusalem so expansive and peaceful as to be without walls and so all-inclusive of every form of life as to teem with a "multitude of men and cattle." Was there confusion—or at least hesitation—in the angelic ranks about the glory and size of the new Jerusalem! Zechariah's Jerusalem reflects the prophetic vision of Second Isaiah, who envisaged a new Jerusalem, "too narrow for your inhabitants" (Isa. 49:19), and who told the people to "let the curtains of your habitations be stretched out, . . . for you will spread abroad to the right and to the left" (Isa. 54:2-3).

The statement about a "wall of fire round about [and] glory within her" (Zech. 2:5) draws upon the remembrance of the protective column of fire in the story of Israel's exodus from a foreign land (Exod. 13:21-22; Deut. 1:33), of Yahweh's presence amid fire on Mount Horeb/Sinai or among the people (Deut. 4:12, 24; Exod. 40:38). It is also possible according to David L. Petersen (*Haggai and Zechariah 1–8*, 171), relying upon D. Stronach, that the prophet's vision of Jerusalem was modeled upon the Persian city of Pasargadae, which had no walls but was adorned with fire altars along its boundaries. The phrase "I will be the glory within her" translates a Hebrew text that may refer much more explicitly to the divine name as spoken by Yahweh to Moses at the burning bush: "I myself am *eheyeh* ("I who am") to her" (Exod. 3:14; cf. Théophane Chary, *Aggée—Zacharie Malachie, 67*).

The RSV translation in Zech. 2:6-7 is uncertain: "Ho! Ho! Flee . . . Ho! Escape to Zion." The Hebrew word *hoy,* translated "Ho," can be traced through a long evolution, back to a practice of wailing and lamenting over great sorrow (1 Kgs. 13:30), into prophetic curses (Amos 5:18), and finally into a sense of "How foolish!" in Isa. 45:9. The meaning in Zechariah is not clear; the NAB translates the phrase with "Up, Up!" Perhaps *hoy* can be paraphrased, "How foolish and how sad [if you do not] flee [and] escape." *Escape to Zion* in the Hebrew text reads without a preposition as an address, "Escape, Zion!" Just as the boundaries of the temple were extended to embrace the entire city of Jerusalem in this vision, likewise the title of Zion is not restricted to the temple, nor even to the wider sweep of the entire holy city (Isa. 1:8) and its inhabitants (Joel 2:23). With Zechariah it is addressed to the people of Israel, wherever they may be, even in the foreign or unclean land of exile (cf. Amos 7:17).

More textual difficulties follow in two disputed phrases in Zech. 2:8, "after his glory sent me" and "touches the apple of his eye." The first is "most puzzling" (Ralph L. Smith, *Micah—Malachi,* 196) and "extremely difficult" (Petersen, 173) with many proposed translations. The second phrase, according to Ernst Würthwein (*The Text of the Old Testament,* 19), is an example of *tiqqune sopherim,* "corrections of the scribes." The prophet meant to say in quoting the words of Yahweh here: "whoever touches Israel touches the pupil of my eye" ('pupil' is a better translation than 'apple'), but to avoid the seemingly blasphemous or at least irreverent thought of touching

Yahweh, the scribes made it read "his eye" (i.e., Israel's). Another example of such a correction is Job 2:9, where the Hebrew text does not read, "Curse God, and die" (RSV) but "Bless God, and die."

In Zech. 2:11 "many nations [are invited to] join themselves to the Lord." This address is to be read in conjunction with another early postexilic declaration:

> And the foreigners who join themselves to the Lord,
>   to minister to him, to love the name of the Lord,
>   and to be his servants,
> every one who keeps the sabbath, . . .
>   and holds fast my covenant—
> these I will bring to my holy mountain,
>   and make them joyful in my house of prayer.
>   (Isa. 56:6-7)

This welcome to foreigners to "join themselves to the Lord" and his people at prayer, represents one side of a double movement towards the Gentiles during the early postexilic period, witnessed even within the prophecy of Zechariah. The prophecy of Zechariah does not lay down the conditions for the admission of Gentiles, whether with dignity (Isa. 56) or in chains (Isa. 45:14). The other side of this movement condemns the nations and separates Israel from them, as in the preceding vision or in Hag. 2:10-14.

The place where all will be assembled is called the "holy land" (Zech. 2:12). This phrase, so commonly in use today, is found elsewhere in the Bible only in the apocrypha (Wis. 12:3; 2 Macc. 1:7). A similar phrase occurred already in Exod. 3:5, referring to the "holy ground" where Moses stood before the burning bush. Zechariah, in some way, is seeing another wondrous vision of the Lord.

"Be silent!" (Zech. 2:13). This phrase summons people to profound reverence within temple liturgy and before cosmic upheavals (Hab. 2:20; Zeph. 1:7). It is not clear if the reference to Yahweh's "holy dwelling" indicates the Jerusalem temple (Pss. 46–48) or the heavenly sanctuary of the Lord (Ps. 29:9-10). Because this passage of Zechariah projects Yahweh's presence with all the people rather than cultically confined to the temple, Yahweh here may be rousing himself and coming from the heavenly abode to descend upon the earth.

THE CERTAINTIES AND UNCERTAINTIES OF PROPHECY

The style of visions alerts us to the *certainties* of God's word (beyond a doubt, from the Lord), which, however, are so thoroughly hidden within the mysteries of God's plans for Israel that they remain *uncertain or vague* for us. Mysteries such as these need not be frustrating, first of all because God is communicating with us by inspired preachers and writers as well as by angelic messengers, and secondly because mystery does not deny the certain reality of God's hopes and plans for us but only reminds us how wondrous they are, beyond our present comprehension.

This conclusion, which can be derived simply from the general format of Zechariah's visions, dominates the dramatic ending of the book of Job, who confesses:

> I have uttered what I did not understand,
> things too wonderful for me,
> which I did not know (Job 42:3).

Similarly, the third vision of Zechariah ends by calling upon us: "Be silent before the LORD" and recognize that all of us are only "flesh," the biblical word for weakness and insecurity. Jeremiah had declared:

> Cursed is the one who trusts in humankind
> and makes *flesh* the arm of strength.
> (Jer. 17:5 author's translation)

Deuteronomy may have prophetic visionaries in mind, when it warned:

> For who is there *of all flesh,* that has heard the voice of the living God speaking out of the midst of fire, as we have, and has still lived? (Deut. 5:26)

The final verse of the third vision moves far along the way to an adequate answer. After calling for silence, the prophet announces that God "has roused himself from his holy dwelling," not to speak a message but *to act* awesomely for Israel's sake. As in Isa. 51:9, where the same Hebrew word is translated "Awake, awake," the Lord is being roused to put on the vesture of battle, "as in days of old [when] thou didst cut Rahab in pieces [and] pierce the dragon." In its ultimate moments, prophecy leads us to a battle in which su-

perhuman forces are locked together and victory comes only
through Yahweh.

God is again roused in another desperate poem, Ps. 44. Israel's armies have fallen in defeat, despite the people's self-assurance that
they have been faithful to the word of the Lord. Almost with in-
solence, the people shout at the Lord:

> Rouse thyself! Why sleepest thou, O LORD?
> Awake! Do not cast us off for ever!
>
> (Ps. 44:23)

This outburst is close to blasphemy, judging from an opposing, clear
statement in Ps. 121:3, "He who keeps Israel will neither slumber
nor sleep." The conclusion of Ps. 44, however, does not leave the
outcome exclusively in the action of Yahweh. Israel too has a part to
play, as it appeals to the Lord: "Deliver us *for the sake of thy steadfast
love!*" The final word, "steadfast love" (Hebrew *hesed*), evokes the
image of blood bond, so sacred in the Near East (Lev. 25:25-55),
with which Israel is united to Yahweh and the consequent obliga-
tions of the nearest of kin are placed upon Yahweh. Bonding in
faithful love rather than in clear messages becomes the ultimate
source of security and divine truth.

Prophecy, therefore, leaves much unsaid and unexplained; the
most important details remain God's secret. As prophecy evolves in
the direction of apocalyptic, visionary literature—a process already
in progress within the fourteen chapters of Zechariah—answers are
fewer, symbols become ever more baffling, and the action of God is
all the more heroic and complex. To repeat ourselves, mystery does
not mean uncertainty in God but rather calls attention to the limits
of our human comprehension. Such mystery evokes the need of a
strong faith and indomitable hope. Eventually, divine action rather
than an inspired message secures our salvation. The message, nonetheless, is the most secure way of preparing us to receive God's redemptive activity.

If we consider the concluding verse of the third vision (Zech.
2:13) in conjunction with two other similar, clearly liturgical passages (Zeph. 1:7; Hab. 2:20), we see another way by which the
mystery of God resolves itself satisfactorily within the cult of Israel.
Each of the other two prophetic pieces are located in a liturgical context: Habakkuk refers to Yahweh in his holy temple and leads at
once to the liturgical hymn comprising ch. 3; Zephaniah likewise
calls for silence "before the Lord God [who] has prepared a sacrifice
and consecrated his guests." If God's word is heard within the con-

text of worship, it blends with music and ceremony and relives many great acts of the Lord *that very moment.* The answer, therefore, to any questions raised by the word of God is to be found in silent worship and the Lord's immediate and active presence, achieving once again the redemption of the people as once in Egypt and again in the wilderness (cf. Deut. 5:1-5; 6:20-25; Josh. 24).

In other stylistic ways the seer in ch. 2 of Zechariah alerts us to the mystery of God within the dilemma of the situation. Visions normally do not open with a straightforward oracle but with a question, generally from the prophet (Zech. 1:9, 19; 2:2; 5:6) or else from the accompanying angel (4:2; 5:2). A second angel is sent, seemingly to insist upon what the first angel may have doubted, that the new Jerusalem is really to be immense and peaceful. Textual problems complicate the mystery, but they are not the prophet's fault; rather, they are due to defective transmission or to our ignorance of Hebrew: (1) the scribal correction in 2:8, lest the language seem too brash in addressing the deity; (2) our quandary in translating v. 5; (3) the enigmatic v. 8.

A more substantive problem remains: the fate of Jerusalem and of the gentile nations. While Jerusalem is to remain without walls under the exclusive protective shield of God's fire, Nehemiah will later return to Jerusalem with the precise mission to rebuild the walls (Neh. 1–7). Nehemiah's action ought not to be interpreted as faithlessness in God's promise in Zechariah, for in writing his annals Nehemiah made no apology, and by faith we accept his book as part of our inspired Scriptures. The solution to our theological problem may lie in politics: building a wall in Zechariah's day would have been interpreted by the Persians as an act of revolt or a stab at independence. There was a practical realism about Zechariah's vision! In Nehemiah's case, the Persians were prevailed upon to grant the necessary permission. The interaction of Persian politics with prophetic oracles was already manifest in the book of Haggai, where God declares at the time of the massive revolts across the Persian Empire, "I will shake the heavens and the earth and the sea and the dry land" (Hag. 2:6, 21). Still earlier Second Isaiah acclaimed another political moment for the fulfillment of prophecy in the victories of Cyrus (Isa. 45:1-7). Nonetheless, it remains religiously embarrassing that theology adapts itself to a political timetable.

The various reactions of prophecy to the salvation of the nations have already been noted in this commentary. While the goal of universal salvation through the God of Israel emerges off and on again, yet there is no systematized development of the position. We can say either that it remained a mystery, locked in the divine counsel—and that is true!—or we can make an equally true, but alternate statement, that this "day of the Lord" was conditioned by the human situation. The history of Christianity witnesses to similar moments when its universal mission was greatly helped or seriously hurt by human actions and decisions within the Church (Acts 10–11; 15; Gal. 2:11-14).

The uncertainties of prophecy, therefore, can be due to mysterious aspects of the revelatory vision before which the reader can only wait in silence before God, until God acts in world history or comes into our midst during community worship; or the uncertainties may be attributed to poor textual transmission. These same perplexities begin to be resolved in a variety of ways: through later revelation (for Christians in Christ Jesus), through human cooperation with God's grace, or through political and economic circumstances in world history.

VISION IV: HIGH PRIEST, PURIFIED AND EXALTED

Zechariah 3:1-10

PRIESTLY "MESSIAH"
AND THE PURIFICATION OF ISRAEL

The fourth of Zechariah's visions breaks the pattern already set by the three preceding ones and to be continued into the next four visions—similar to the way that the final vision in Amos 9:1-4 does not follow the sequence of those in Amos 7:1-9 and 8:1-3. We miss the introductory formula and the question of the prophet; the messenger or angel of the Lord, as David L. Petersen points out, is not an "interlocutor or interpreter for Zechariah [but] works exclusively within the visionary world" (*Haggai and Zechariah 1–8*, 190).

The vision is presented in Zech. 3:1-5, its explanation in vv. 6-10. The setting is the heavenly council where Yahweh is surrounded by other spirits or servants, one of whom is an *adversary* of Israel or humankind, as the Hebrew name *Satan* means. We are reminded particularly of Job 1:6-12; 2:1-6, where Satan disputes with Yahweh about the genuine righteousness of God's servant, Job. In still other biblical vignettes of God's throne room, the place is inhabited by spirits obedient to the Lord but nonetheless hostile at times to people on earth: i.e., 1 Kgs. 22:19-23 and Ps. 82. At other times they praise the glory of Yahweh (Ps. 29:1, 9-10) and are ever prompt to do the divine will (Isa. 6). The statues of the cherubim (or "seraphim" according to Isaiah) on either side of the ark of the covenant mirror in the earthly temple what was happening in the heavenly temple (Exod. 25:18-22; 40:34-36; 1 Kgs. 8:6), just as the dwelling of God in the holy of holies of the Jerusalem temple was an extension of God's paramount presence in the heavenly sanctuary (Deut. 12:11; Ps. 150).

The preceding vision left us in silence before the Lord in the celestial sanctuary (Zech. 2:13). This final verse of ch. 2 prepares us to meet the high priest Joshua (see the explanatory notes with Hag. 1:1-14), standing before the Lord in the midst of the heavenly court. He is about to be purified and then invested with royal privileges. Zerubbabel, heir to the Davidic promises, seems to have passed from the scene (see Zech. 6:9-14), and his role has been subsumed under the high priest, who is priest and king like Melchizedek (Gen. 14:18-20; Ps. 110:4). Previously, kings controlled the sanctuary and occasionally functioned as priests (1 Kgs 3:3-15); now the high priest will act in both a civil and a religious capacity. The prophet Ezekiel had already insisted upon the exclusive rights of the Zadokite priests over all other Levites (Ezek. 40:46; 44:10-31), ranking the priest even higher than the prince (Ezek. 46:2, avoiding the title of "king"). Zechariah will focus ever more exclusively upon the high priest.

The dialogue in Zech. 3:2 records a serious conflict: "The LORD said to Satan, 'The Lord rebuke you, O Satan!'" This literal translation of the RSV from the Hebrew text probably ought to be amended to read, "The *messenger of* the Lord said to Satan" (cf. Petersen, 186-87). The Hebrew text, nonetheless, reflects the frequency with which "angel" or "celestial spirit" merges with Yahweh (i.e., Exod. 3:1-6). The Hebrew word for "rebuke" (*ga'ar*) generally indicates strong, even at times violent action (Isa. 50:2; 51:20; 54:9), as must be the case in the struggle here between goodness and evil, now on a cosmic scale with the future of Israel in the balance. It is the Lord who rebukes, challenges, and reverses the desires of Satan. Even though the purification is cast here in a sanctuary or liturgical setting, nonetheless, at key moments the exclusive role of the Lord in saving the high priest and the people emerges clearly. See the section below for a further discussion of angels, demons, and pneumatology. The words about the high priest, "a brand plucked from the fire," repeat Amos 4:11 almost verbatim, so that we are dealing with a proverb from a common treasury of speech. While Amos is referring to all Israel, Zechariah thinks of the high priest, Israel's representative, who bears the people's guilt and who narrowly escapes from Satan.

Clothing, especially of prominent people like king and high priest, was highly symbolical in Israel and was identifiable with the person and the office (1 Sam. 18:3-4; 24:4-5). With sacred or distinctive vestments priests assumed office and functioned in the sanctuary (Exod. 28–29; Lev. 21:10; Sir. 45:7-12; 50:11). Prophets too were recognizable by their mantle and transferred authority by this means (Zech. 13:4; 1 Kgs. 19:19; 2 Kgs. 2:8, 13-15). The action in the fourth vision, therefore, concerns the high priest as the people's representative in worship before God. Personal and corporate sins are brought before God by the high priest in begging for divine forgiveness, as on the Day of Atonement (Lev. 16). It is not that ritual forgives sin; only God grants that grace. A passage like Num. 5:5-10 lays out the conditions for absolution from sin and readmission to the assembly of worship and life: confessing one's fault to the neighbor who has been harmed and admitting that one has broken "faith with the Lord"; restoring stolen goods plus 20 percent; and finally a ritual action at the temple to *signify* the guilty person's new purity before the Lord and the community. The first two actions prepare a person for forgiveness; the ritual action celebrates this forgiveness, removing all suspicion and guilt and receiving the once guilty person within the assembly of worship. This ceremony may be reflected in Pss. 15 and 24.

"Filthy" is an exceptionally graphic word for describing the high priest's garments. It generally indicates clothing or place befouled with human excrement (Deut. 23:13; Ezek. 4:12; Isa. 28:8; 36:12). "Rich, clean turban" indicates a symbolic reinstatement of the high priest and symbolically of all Israel. The turban or cloth that is wound around the high priest's head befits an eminent person (Isa. 62:3; Job 29:14), who is now "clean," and according to the Hebrew word *tahor,* no longer a contagious source of evil and disease in the community.

In the explanation of the vision, the high priest is to "walk in my ways and keep my charge" (Zech. 3:7). The words are all inclusive of godly living, highlighting moral rectitude (Deut. 8:6; 10:12-13) and ritual correctness (Num. 3). The high priest is granted "right of access" to divine intimacy and to a place within the celestial court, "standing here" in God's presence. Joshua and the other priests are addressed as "men of good omen"; they are signs like the children of Isaiah (Isa. 8:18). Through liturgical vestments and ceremony they express not only the hopes of the people but also their own immediate absorption into the wonders of God. They are now given titles formerly reserved to the Davidic royalty, "my servant the Branch" (Isa. 11:1; Jer. 23:5; Ezek. 17:22-24; Hag. 2:23). These titles either enhance the "messianic" role of the priest, or at least bestow upon the priest the role of tutor and guardian of the future royal messiah.

The text declares in Zech. 3:9 that a "single stone with seven facets" and "inscription" is placed before the high priest. The passage is variously explained: (1) the gem worn in the high priest's turban or the gold plate worn over the breast, engraved with a seven letter Hebrew inscription, "Holy to the Lord—*qds yhwh*" (Exod. 28:36-38); (2) the rock of sacrifice, upon which according to the Targum on Exod. 28:20 and Eccl. 3:11 was inscribed the name of

Yahweh (Théophane Chary, *Les prophètes et le culte à partir de l'exil,*
149-151); or (3) according to an alternate yet acceptable translation, "seven springs" of water, flowing from the altar of sacrifice
(Ezek. 47:1-12; Zech. 14:8). The third variation is inspired by
Moses' striking the rock for water in the wilderness (Exod. 17:6;
Num. 20:8), a rock that followed the Israelites in the desert (1 Cor.
10:4). This explanation, advanced by Edward Lipiński (*VT*
20 [1970]: 25-29), translates the Hebrew word for "facets"
('enayim) as "springs," actually a more common meaning of the
word. Typical of symbolism, particularly of Semitic vintage, a single
word can have various meanings at once; symbols are not so much
intended to give answers and to close discussion as to open up new
perceptions and to lead us reflectively, perhaps mystically, into the
wonders of God's presence and hopes for us.

The account ends with everyone inviting the neighbor to recline
"under his vine and under his fig tree." The image is typical of peace,
especially the peace of the new, messianic age (1 Kgs. 4:25; 2 Kgs.
18:31; Mic. 4:4; John 1:48). Through temple liturgy Israel is surrounded with the paradise of the messianic age—an idea to be developed much further in the apocryphal book of Sirach, ch. 24.

FROM PROPHECY AND ROYALTY TO PRIESTHOOD

By highlighting the role of the high priest, the vision stresses ceremonial acts at the temple for arriving at purity in God's eyes. Prophecy, which formerly demanded social justice as the condition to be
forgiven one's sins (Isa. 1:2-17; Jer. 7), now tilts the scale in the
other direction towards the accompanying ritual acts.

Implied as well in the preceding observations on this fourth vision was the way by which the role of the messiah of the royal house
of David was eclipsed and another side of messianism is accented,
that of the priesthood. It is too early to say that Zechariah was announcing a priestly messiah of the house of Aaron, as we find among
the Dead Sea Scrolls (1QS 9:11). Perhaps it may be better, at this
point of theological development, to speak of "messianism without
a messiah," that is, without human instrumentality and directly by
Yahweh—as announced in the preaching of the exilic prophet Second Isaiah (Isa. 40–55), or later in the postexilic psalms that honor
Yahweh as king (Pss. 96–99). While priesthood was certainly being
enhanced, it was also being absorbed within the glorious presence of
Yahweh in the temple and its ritual. Such a delicate equilibrium is always difficult for priesthood or any kind of religious ministry to

maintain: to be God's instruments for leading people into the presence of God and representing them before God without claiming divine prerogatives for oneself!

ANGELS, DEMONS, AND PNEUMATOLOGY

The fourth vision of Zechariah (ch. 3) raises another theological question, enabling us to study the evolution of Israel's belief in spirits, good and evil, angels and devils. At first the distinction is not clearly drawn between God and other superhuman spirits. Early passages about the "angel of the Lord," as in the incident of the burning bush (Exod. 3), begin by speaking of "the angel of the Lord [who] appeared to Moses in a flame of fire out of the midst of a bush"; yet once Moses seeks to identify the angelic speaker, the voice replies, "I am the God of your ancestors." Similarly in Gen. 18 the Lord seems to blend into the person of "the three men [who] stood in front of" Abraham, and yet in v. 17 God steps away from them and speaks separately and distinctly.

In other examples angels are called "host of heaven" (1 Kgs. 22:19), "heavenly beings" who form "the council of the holy ones" (Ps. 89:6-7), "children of the gods" (Ps. 29:1), or simply "gods" (a possible translation of Ps. 8:5). These passages represent a strong influence from neighboring religions. Sometimes these other "gods" are taken seriously, to be combatted by Yahweh (Ps. 89:9; Isa. 51:9-10) or else to be allocated to the lot of other nations (Deut. 4:19; 32:8-9). The references are not clear and can be interpreted metaphorically for God's battle against hostile world powers.

Only in the literature of a prophet like Zechariah do angels begin to appear in a separate role as independent beings. At the same time, then, when God is becoming ever more transcendent and awesome (if we compare the impression of God left with us from Zechariah or Job with that in Gen. 18), the distance between God and the people is bridged by intermediary spirits called angels who share in God's government of the universe.

The negative side of biblical theology always develops more slowly than the positive, and so the understanding of demons and Satan took still more time than that of angels. In some early passages Satan expresses "God's anger [which] was kindled because [Balaam] went [with the elders of Moab and Midian]; and the angel of the Lord took his stand in the way as his adversary [literally, as his 'satan']" (Num. 22:22). Satan can be any kind of adversary, obedient to Yahweh but hostile to humankind.

In another series of texts, Satan shows up in the throne room of Yahweh, ready and even anxious to undertake a mission against the welfare of Israel or other people: Zech. 3:1; Job 1–2; 1 Chr. 21:1. The last of these passages reads, "Satan stood up against Israel, and incited David to number Israel." It is helpful to compare it with its earlier source in 2 Sam. 24:1, "Again *the anger of the LORD* was kindled against Israel, and he incited David against them, saying, 'Go, number Israel and Judah.'" The former passage of 1 Chr. 21:1, coming at a later time, puts more theological refinement into the statement of 2 Sam. 24:1!

The Greek LXX, especially in Wis. 2:24, identifies Satan with the serpent of Gen. 3; and similarly it translates Zech. 3:1 as *diabolos.*

The Bible, therefore, struggled a long time to express adequately the strong faith that Yahweh is ever present, accomplishing the divine will, whether it be in favorable or hostile situations. Earlier, all mysterious actions and spirits were seen in God or around the throne of God; in later periods evil is separate from God, though still mysteriously enough within the purpose and plan of God. This mystery could not be solved, even within the forty-two chapters of Job, and the NT continues to baffle us, as in the temptation scene of Jesus (Matt. 4:1-11; Mark 1:12-13; Luke 4:1-13).

VISION V: THE TWO ANOINTED ONES

Zechariah 4:1-14

THEOLOGICAL CONCLUSIONS
FROM BIBLICAL DIFFICULTIES

Strange and awkward as it may seem as a way for doing theology, yet the many difficulties that plague the scholar in this chapter of the prophecy of Zechariah provide a basis for important theological conclusions. Our reasoning is based on the position of faith that the Bible, as the foundation of our belief and practice, is the Bible as received from Israel and the early Church. Our explanations need to flow primarily from *this* Bible rather than from its earlier traditions (i.e., the four traditions of the Pentateuch—the Yahwist, Elohist, Priestly, or Deuteronomic) or even from the earliest preaching of the prophet Zechariah. Much of it may not have been recorded; what we possess generally amounts to edited fragments. The editor was basically true to the prophet's original message, yet as a person of reason and as someone with a pastoral sense to his or her own day, the editor was not above adaptation and rearrangement. It is important to seek the reasons why the editor gave a particular shape to the overall message. This shaping of the earlier preaching may confuse the historical occasion of Zechariah's preaching with the situation of the later editor. The editor, however, by his work is advising us to adapt or apply this material to our context in order that the message of the prophet may have an impact upon our contemporary life for prayer, justice, and peace.

We do not know whether to ascribe the situation to the prophet Zechariah or to the editor (probably the latter), but many *literary and textual questions* face us in ch. 4. There is a serious interruption in the flow of thought at vv. 6-10. The problem becomes all the more evident from scanning the Hebrew text, where vv. 1-5 and 11-14 are printed in block prose while vv. 6-10 follow a poetic arrangement of lines.

While there is general agreement that an addition was made to the original form of the vision-narrative, nonetheless there is very little consensus among scholars and translators in dealing with the situation. The RSV divides v. 10 and keeps the first half of it with the poetic addition and the second half with the vision as described in prose within vv. 1-5 and 11-14. The NAB places vv. 4-10 immediately after ch. 3 as a continuation of the fourth vision. Still other suggestions are put forward. If our faith and theological reflections depend upon the Scriptures *as handed down in Jewish and Christian tradition,* then first attention should be given the purpose of the final editor who stitched the poetry of vv. 6-10 into the prose narrative of the vision. Verses 6-10 stress the importance of rebuilding the temple as a way of overcoming the lethargy of "the day of small things"; they necessarily highlight the role of Zerubbabel of the Davidic family, who sanctioned and furthered this construction. Whatever be the bleak future of the dynasty in the postexilic age, it has given Israel—through its representative Zerubbabel—a central base to keep the people united before God and strong in their perseverance to God's promises to them. Humanly speaking, whatever be the faults of the dynasty, it has been God's instrument in rebuilding the temple and so in preserving Israel and its religion for us today.

As we look more closely at this chapter, still other textual difficulties emerge. To cite some of them helps in detecting an aspect of visionary and apocalyptic literature, important for theological conclusions. While v. 2 refers to "seven lamps . . . with seven lips [or spouts] on each" (the Hebrew text is disturbed with another 'seven' dangling loose), v. 10 speaks instead of "seven . . . *eyes,*" which can also be translated "seven . . . *fountains.*" In 3:9 we saw that "seven facets" can also be translated "seven fountains" or "seven eyes." Eyes as flowing in tears provide the background for the sense of "fountains." Zech. 4:7, moreover, shows many rough edges in the literal Hebrew reading: "Who are you, O great mountain? Before Zerubbabel [you become] a plain. He will bring forth the capstone—shouts to it of 'Grace! Grace!'" (author's translation). The ancient Greek and Syriac have still other readings!

By keeping v. 10b united with the poetic additions (vv. 6-10), against the RSV arrangement, then the results of Zerubbabel's temple will "range through the whole earth" (v. 10b). If we keep the RSV translation of "eyes," then from the temple the Lord will plan and care for the earth; if we prefer the translation "fountains," then the fresh water, flowing from the Lord's presence in the temple, will spread fertility across the earth. Ralph L. Smith (*Micah—Malachi,* 203) reminds us that the Hebrew verb here for "range" is used for flood waters in later Hebrew (cf. Isa. 28:15, 18; Job 9:23) and therefore signifies the mighty cleansing power of this water, as the Lord speaks words of justice and forgiveness in the prophetic preaching at the temple.

An archaeological difficulty confronts us in the central item of the vision:

> a lampstand all of gold, with a bowl on the top of it, and seven lamps on it, with seven lips [or spouts] on each of the lamps which are on top of it. (Zech. 4:2)

This description does not correspond to the golden lampstand in Exod. 25:31-40 and 37:17-24. Solomon's temple, moreover, had *ten* lampstands of pure gold (cf. 1 Kgs. 7:49), while the number was reduced again to one in the temple of 1 Macc. 1:21. The description in Exodus agrees with the seven-branched lampstand inscribed on the arch of Titus in Rome, where the emperor commemorated his victory over the Jews and the loot taken from the Jerusalem temple in A.D. 70. However, the many lampstands unearthed in places in and around Israel, at Ugarit, Dan, Gezer, Akko, and Lachish, dating from the fifteenth to the eighth centuries B.C., provide a better idea of what appeared in Zechariah's vision. A single shaft of twisted or spiral columns supported a large bowl, on whose outer rim in turn were placed seven small bowls. Each of the latter was pinched in seven places to provide a place for seven wicks.

The uncertainty about the relation of this lampstand with traditional ones mentioned elsewhere in the Bible is matched by the ambiguity about the overall symbolism. Most scholars think that the lampstand announces the presence of Yahweh in the Jerusalem temple. Yet when we read Zech. 4:10b, "these seven are the eyes of the Lord, which range through the whole earth," some authors consider this a reference to the people Israel, who beam a message of truth and justice to the nations (cf. Isa. 51:4), an image continued in the NT (cf. Matt. 5:14-16), and especially in the book of Revelation, where "the seven lampstands are the seven churches" (Rev. 1:20). Here then is still another interpretation of the "seven eyes" or "seven fountains," already discussed above.

We note the ease with which the Bible blends water and light (cf. Ps. 36:8-9; 68:8-9; Zech. 14:6-8). Not only is each life-giving, but rainwater so cleanses the atmosphere that light floods the earth. In Christian tradition the Easter vigil service combines light and water, the light of Christ illumines and washes one in the water of baptism.

We are faced again with *the historical problem* of sorting out the roles of Joshua the high priest and Zerubbabel the governor: (1) in the preceding vision the high priest absorbed the role of civil administration; (2) here we notice that in the prose narrative of the vision the two anointed ones, the priest and the governor, are given equal attention; (3) with the poetic account in vv. 6-10 Zerubbabel and his role in rebuilding the temple are the exclusive center of concern. Incidentally, the symbolism is again confusing: the two are pictured as two olive trees (v. 3), later as "two branches of the olive trees," or as "two golden pipes" (v. 12). We can extrapolate from the confusion, however, the position of Haggai and that adopted at first in Zechariah, that the high priest and the governor work together. This fifth vision represents an earlier view of Zechariah, the fourth vision a later settlement upon the sole prerogative of the high priest.

AWAKENED OUT OF SLEEP

Ambiguity such as we have been encountering in ch. 4 leads to a rather certain feature of visionary accounts, and especially of apocalyptic writing whose forerunner is seen in Zech. 1-8: the vision does not so much impart a clear message as it inspires long reflection and most of all induces a new strength and composure in the Lord. While it may confuse scholars that the lampstand refers to several different traditional forms without being restricted to any single one of them, the prophet is settling the reader in a liturgical tradition as ancient as Moses and Solomon and as contemporary as his own day. The reader (or for those times, the listener) is asked to contemplate what defies clear lines of imagination and theology. One is drawn into what Christian mystics call the dark night of the senses and of the spirit; here one experiences an overwhelming, blinding presence of God's light. It is not that a confusing picture is drawn by the prophet but rather that God explodes our human limitations. The psalmist wrote:

> If I say, "Let only darkness cover me,
>   and the light about me be night,"
> even the darkness is not dark to thee,
>   the night is bright as the day;
>   for darkness is as light with thee.
>   (Ps. 139:11-12)

As we look into the night, we must heed the call of the angel to be awakened from our sleep (Zech. 4:1, the only time when this phrase occurs in the visions of Zechariah) and not to despise but rather to rejoice in "the day of small things" (v. 10). We gather as people of faith who worship together in the temple built by the Spirit, and we are guided by the branches of the olive tree, our leaders, who receive their rich instruction from the golden lampstand of "the Lord of the whole earth" (v. 14).

Zerubbabel and Joshua are the source of rich olive oil to the people Israel; they are "the two golden pipes from which the oil is poured out" (v. 12). From them comes an abundant fertility throughout the land, as indicated in an unusual Hebrew word for "oil," which literally means "gold[en oil]," the very finest for taste and good health. High priest and governor, or in the poetic account the governor alone, are seen exclusively in reference to the temple, and the temple exclusively in terms of the wondrous and fruitful presence of God. These two leaders first need to be chosen and consecrated by the Lord (cf. v. 14, "the two anointed who stand by the Lord of the whole earth"). As was said of Zerubbabel at the end of the prophecy of Haggai, he is "my servant [whom] I have chosen" (Hag. 2:23).

Because they are God's servants and instruments, Zerubbabel especially is to accomplish his goal, "not by might, nor by power, but by my Spirit, says the Lord of hosts" (v. 6). Zerubbabel is not like Solomon commanding an army of workers (cf. 1 Kgs. 5:13-15) nor like Nehemiah with a corps of load-carriers (cf. Neh. 4:10; Joyce Baldwin, *Haggai, Zechariah, Malachi,* 121). While in the books of Joshua and Judges the Spirit of God enabled military leaders to be victorious in war (cf. Judg. 3:10; 6:34; 7:2; 13:25; 14:6), and in the story of the charismatic prophets to be stirred with feverish enthusiasm and even to be turned into "another person," hardly recognizable even to themselves (cf. 1 Sam. 10:5-6), here in the prophecy of Zechariah the Spirit of the Lord has a gentle way of achieving wondrous results, as in Isaiah 11.

In quarrying material for rebuilding the temple, the "great mountain [of stone] . . . shall become a plain," a symbolic way of underlining abundance of material and the "splendor of this house . . . greater than the former" (Hag. 2:9). When the final stone is put in place, there are shouts of "Grace, grace!" (Zech. 4:7), something very pleasing to the eye. Some interpret the mountain as the strong opposition to Zerubbabel's rebuilding of the temple, either from neighboring people of the land (cf. Ezra 4:4; 5:3-5), or from mean-spirited Jews who were ridiculing Zerubbabel and reducing everything to a "day of small things" (Zech. 4:10). Smith remarks (206): "The idea of moving mountains of opposition to the kingdom of

God is prominent in the NT (Matt. 17:20; 21:21-22; Mark 11:22-23; Luke 17:6; 1 Cor. 13:2)." The last passage from 1 Corinthians warns us, however, that unless such faith is suffused with love, "I am nothing."

No matter how careful the work and how inspired the spirit, nothing will hold together until the top stone is put in place (Zech. 4:7). Many biblical passages come to mind here, each blending their own distinct message into the contemplation of the passage of Zechariah:

> Isa. 28:16, where God is "laying in Zion for a foundation a stone, a tested stone, a precious cornerstone, of a sure foundation: 'He who believes will not be in haste.'" Here the cornerstone seems to be the faith infused by God in the heart of the people.

> Ps. 118:22-23, where the Lord is doing something marvelous, "the stone which the builders rejected has become the head of the corner." In this case the stone may be the people Israel, once rejected, still very insignificant, yet nonetheless the object of the Lord's beneficence. In the NT the cornerstone is Jesus, the new temple, the gathering place for worship in spirit and in truth (Matt. 21:42; Acts 4:11; 1 Pet. 2:7).

These references modulate the image from the top stone that holds the arch together to the cornerstone upon which the building rests. Each, in any case, is essential for the structure to stay in place. These biblical passages raise another serious theological question. At first reading they seem to imply that God sends great suffering, like the Exile and in NT times the destruction of Jerusalem, as a means of purifying Israel and of leading Israel to the next important stage of history. Such an inference produces an image of a cruel God. Again we cannot form our theology of God nor of God's providential care of Israel from any single series of biblical texts, and in this case we need to look to other passages about God's compassionate and forgiving love: i.e., Exod. 34; Hos. 11:8-9; Isa. 54.

As we peer into the night, the light of God comes to us from many biblical directions. Before and after the time of Zechariah God insisted upon the importance of the temple for the continuity of Israel and upon the unconditional need of faith and charity if the temple was to survive. Religious and civil leadership are recognized for their crucial role in supporting the structure of the temple. Yet they too will collapse unless they realize that the Lord is the source of their choice, their anointing, and their wisdom. With the Lord's support they will level every mountain and overcome all opposition; without the Lord they will cease to exist as happened to the temple in 587 B.C. and will happen again in A.D. 70.

THE LAST THREE VISIONS: PURITY AND READINESS FOR TEMPLE RECONSTRUCTION
Zechariah 5:1–6:8

STRUCTURE AND LIFE FROM ANCIENT ROOTS

The final three visions move quickly to a conclusion that all is ready for the return of the exiles and the reconstruction of the temple. The order of the first three visions is repeated in reverse (Joyce G. Baldwin, *Haggai, Zechariah, Malachi*, 80-81). Vision VI announces the removal of guilt from Jerusalem to Babylon, while Vision III describes the new, glorious Jerusalem. Vision VII corresponds to Vision II, for each sets out to purify and strengthen Jerusalem. The first vision and the eighth or final one have many parallels, beginning with the four multicolored horses and concluding with the idea of rest.

The general literary pattern for all visions (except for the fourth) occurs here: an introduction, a description of what is being seen, the prophet's question, and last of all an explanation from the angelic messenger.

While some nonbiblical imagery is woven into the narrative of these final visions (i.e., in 6:1, the likeness of two bronze mountains from which heavenly chariots emerge is found on Babylonian seals), the major source of the prophet's symbols is biblical: i.e., the length and breadth of the scroll in the sixth vision (5:2) follow the same dimensions as the vestibule of Solomon's temple (1 Kgs. 6:3); not only is a scroll frequently mentioned as we approach the time of the Exile (Jer. 36:2, 32), but one inscribed with woes and mourning is mentioned in Ezek. 2:10–3:2; the heavenly being with wings in the seventh vision (Zech. 5:9) reminds us of the inaugural visions of Isaiah and Ezekiel (Isa. 6:2; Ezek. 1:6); the wind is extolled as a servant of God in Zech. 6:5 as well as in Ps. 104:3-4.

There are many differences in Israel's new covenant with the Lord after the Exile and settlement in the land as compared with the Sinaitic covenant during the pioneer days under Moses and the first settlement in the land under Moses' successor, Joshua. Zechariah,

nonetheless, finds it necessary to stress a continuous bond with
tradition, and as we shall see, a firm rooting in the Mosaic covenant.

Particularly in Vision VI, echoes of the prophetic call for social
justice are heard again. Prophecy has evolved in significant ways. A
new climate and environment have induced many changes necessary
for survival. The growth, nonetheless, has been steady, and all the
while prophecy was reaching to its ancient roots for life and nourishment.

VISION VI: THE FLYING SCROLL (5:1-4)

The central idea is clear enough: the letters on the scroll are too large
ever to be ignored or mistaken. A flying scroll enunciates the quick-
ness and thoroughness with which sin is condemned and removed.
We are reminded of the prophet Habakkuk's answer from the Lord:

> Write the vision;
> make it plain upon tablets
> so one may read it on the run.
> (Hab. 2:2 author's translation)

The scroll is not rolled up and placed within the ark or in some other
safe place; rather, it is unrolled plainly for all to read (Joyce G.
Baldwin, *Haggai, Zechariah, Malachi*, 126).

Through a possible wordplay the scroll (Hebrew *megillah*) is
closely identified with its message of curse (Hebrew *'alah*). In biblical tradition curses were meant to seek out the unknown perpetra-
tor of a crime (Judg. 17:2), to establish if a crime was committed or
not (Num. 5:21-28, in the case of adultery), and especially to punish
a breach of a treaty or covenant. In the latter case, the reading of
Gen. 26:28 is significant, for we see how "curse" can carry another
meaning like "oath" or "covenant": "Let there be an oath *('alah)* between you and us, and let us make a covenant with you." Curse and
covenant are identified, one word stressing the bonding of the par-
ties, the other word insisting upon its seriousness and the punish-
ments for any infraction of it. Deut. 29, moreover, introduces the
word *'alah* nine times in a covenant context, i.e.,

> The anger of the LORD and his jealousy would smoke against
> that person, and the *curses* written in the book would settle
> upon him, and the LORD would blot out his name from under
> heaven . . . in accordance with all the curses of the covenant
> written in the book of the law. (vv. 20-21 author's translation)

The curse can exonerate the innocent peson, as in the case of the ordeal of the suspected adulterous person (Num. 5:21-28), or it can be followed by a blessing for the repentant thief who restores the stolen property (Judg. 17:2). The curse, however, is a final, most serious, albeit compassionate warning. It clearly announces the last chance: either repent or suffer the severe consequences!

Like prophecy in all stages of its evolution, Zechariah combines a strong zeal for social justice with the covenant. He excoriates everyone who swears by God's name—falsely it has to be—and then steals from the neighbor. Three times the word "house" is employed, leading up to the destruction of the house (Zech. 5:4), at a time when the house of the Lord is being reconstructed. Unless a family's house mirrors the holiness of the house of the Lord, it will collapse. Zechariah mentions two sins that violate an injunction on each of the two tablets of the law, one of which represents sins against the Lord (Exod. 20:7, "You shall not take the name of the LORD your God in vain") and sins against one's neighbor (Exod. 20:15, "You shall not steal").

VISION VII: THE FLYING EPHAH (5:5-11)

Following in the wake of the preceding vision, this one removes all doubt whether or not sin, especially cheating the poor or the innocent with false scales and measurements, has been completely removed. Sin, symbolized by a woman, is thrust into an ephah, a container for measuring grain and other dry goods (Ruth 2:17), and a lid of leaden weight seals off its opening. Sin and punishment are carefully measured and securely removed. An ephah, like other weights and measurements in ancient Israel, is difficult to determine, somewhere between 3/8 to 2/3 of a U.S. bushel, 23-36 litres. It is clearly too small for containing a human being, and therefore is used here for its symbolic value.

Because measurements were frequently determined in makeshift ways (a common rock on one side of the balance scale), cheating was an easy temptation to the wily merchant. The Bible frequently speaks of the *just* ephah: e.g.,

> You shall not have in your bag two kinds of weights, a large and a small. You shall not have in your house two kinds of measures, a large and a small. A full and just weight [and] measure you shall have; that your days may be prolonged in the land which the LORD your God gives you. For all . . . who

act dishonestly, are an abomination to the LORD your God. (Deut. 25:13-15)

Shall I acquit the man with wicked scales and with a bag of deceitful weights? (Mic. 6:11)

Zechariah's prophetic defense of honesty is intensified in its seriousness when we recall from the fourth vision (Zech. 3) that the high priest Joshua had already been ritually cleansed of his and the people's sins. Whatever be the liturgical action, sin remains until social justice is achieved.

Not necessarily to Zechariah's honor according to modern standards of sexual discrimination, yet following in a long biblical tradition, woman typifies evil. This practice is quite evident in the prophecy of Hosea, where his adulterous wife Gomer (not her lovers!) stands in for Israel's guilt. This choice of a female symbol is especially blatant when the object of the symbol is found in the licentious and greedy priests and rulers, certainly of the male sex (cf. Hos. 4:4-10; 5:1-4). This practice of symbolizing sin in the person of a woman continues in NT times, not only in public outrage against prostitutes with little or no attention to their customers, as when only "a woman . . . caught in adultery" was brought to Jesus (John 8:3-4), but also in 1 Tim. 2:14, "Adam was not deceived, but the woman was deceived and became a transgressor," and in 2 Cor. 11:3, "I am afraid that as the serpent deceived Eve by his cunning, your thoughts will be led astray . . ." The kindliest interpretation to this one-sided, symbolic appraisal of the origins of sin is given by Théophane Chary: "Thus evil has a face" (*Aggée—Zacharie Mala-chie*, 103), and so is not reduced to words and theories.

A house or temple is built in Babylon for the ephah and the sinful woman. The returnees in Israel, now that all impurities have been removed, can readily proceed to rebuild their own house for God. Zechariah employs the ancient name Shinar for Babylon, found in the early chapters of Genesis, Gen. 10:10 and especially 11:2 where it is associated with the Tower of Babel and the division of the human race into sinful, jealous, and hostile factions. A new unity is possible through the Jerusalem temple that reverses the curse upon the human race at the Tower of Babel (cf. Zech. 2:6-13).

VISION VIII: THE FOUR CHARIOTS (6:1-8)

The preceding vision leaves the ephah in sinful Babylon; this vision begins in that country with a Babylonian image of two bronze mountains, gateways to the divine dwelling in the heavens. Four chariots sally forth from this entrance. In biblical tradition, moreover, mountains are frequently the primary dwelling place of God:

> Great is the Lord . . . in the city of our God!
> His holy mountain, beautiful in elevation,
>   is the joy of all the earth,
> Mount Zion, in the far north,
>   the city of the great King.
>
>   (Ps. 48:1-2)

Comparing this vision with the first, we find similarities and differences. This one opens with the mountains before us, the first vision with a deep valley. The color of the horses forms a link between the first and final visions of Zechariah.

We learn from 1 Kgs. 10:26-29 that Solomon imported finely crafted chariots from Egypt and well-bred horses from Cicilia or Kue in the southwest coast of Asia Minor, not only for his own military adventures but also for resale as a middleman to other neighboring countries. Chariots took on a religious symbolism (2 Kgs. 23:11; Ps. 19:5-6).

The presence in the temple of chariots for the sun and for the cherubim beside the ark of the covenant (1 Chr. 28:18; Ezek. 1) easily led to the association of chariots with the four winds of the heavens and consequently the appreciation of Yahweh as "the Lord of all the earth." The Bible frequently enough mentions the "spirits" (another way other than "wind" for translating Hebrew *ruah*) who form the Lord's retinue in the heavenly sanctuary (1 Kgs. 22:19-23; Job 1:6; 2:1; see also Zechariah's fourth vision, ch. 3). The four winds or spirits serve "the Lord of all the earth . . . and patrol the earth" (6:5, 7). We stand in awe at the universal sweep of the Lord's domain and power. Jeremiah speaks of "the four winds from the four quarters of heaven [through which the Lord] will scatter" Israel's enemy, Elam (Jer. 49:36). Ezekiel summoned "the four winds [to] breathe upon these slain [of Israel in exile], that they may live" (Ezek. 37:9).

"The picture," as David L. Petersen writes, "is one that creates confidence in the world order" (*Haggai and Zechariah 1-8*, 270), completely under the Lord's control and, it is important to add, for the sake of Israel.

It is difficult to decide if the colors of the horses should be pressed for a symbolic meaning. From Rev. 6:1-8 and other apocalyptic texts we learn that red indicates war or martyrdom, white stands for victory, black for famine, and dappled or pale or sorrel (here the Hebrew word of Zechariah is uncertain) for death. A careful study of the first vision and this final one leaves the question open. Others, like Petersen (263, 270-71), prefer to see here a reference exclusively to the four corners of the globe; this minimal interpretation is certainly supported by the statement about "the four winds of heaven."

In any case, Zechariah, as a forerunner of the apocalyptic movement, subscribes to the latter's theology on war and pacifism: whatever is to be achieved lies exclusively in God's hands. These texts are by no means an endorsement of human warfare, much less of nuclear battles that will blow up all four corners of the earth. Nor does Zechariah advocate rebellion. As with Haggai, it is the Lord who "will shake the heavens and the earth and the sea and the dry land" (Hag. 2:6). The work of the Lord's instruments, Joshua and Zerubbabel, is confined to rebuilding the temple and purifying the nation Israel of social injustices.

One of the most frequently used words in the last three visions is "go forth, proceed" (Hebrew *yatsa'*), in Zech. 5:3, 4, 5 (twice), 6, 9; 6:1, 5, 6 (twice), 7, 8. The scene, therefore, stirs with strenuous activity in all directions, as the Lord prepares the entire universe for Israel's return to its own land and for the construction of the new temple at Jerusalem.

While the first vision concludes with a statement from the four horsemen: "we have patrolled the earth, and behold, all the earth remains *at rest*" (1:11), this vision concludes with the steeds "impatient to get off and patrol the earth" and with the Lord's "Spirit *at rest* in the north country." Yahweh is ever ready to defend the people Israel and their temple against invaders from any of the four corners of the earth. Almost like the steeds, the Lord is straining at the bit, at rest not so much in doing nothing as in the realization that the divine plans for the people Israel are in good hands.

The land is purified, the evil forces of the world are subdued, and the temple is ready for the service of the Lord. It will mirror on earth the heavenly sanctuary; Israelites will function like the spirits before the heavenly throne.

CONCLUSION TO THE VISIONS
Zechariah 6:9-15

The eighth and final vision ended with the Lord's resting in peaceful control of the universe after, in the seventh vision, the holy city of Jerusalem had been purified and its curse carried off to Babylon. To wrap things up, the editor now speaks of Jewish exiles coming in steady stream from Babylon to support the Jerusalem temple. This universal convergence upon the temple links up carefully with the first and third visions, wherein Jerusalem and the neighboring cities are said to "overflow with prosperity" (1:17) as "many nations shall join themselves to the Lord" (2:11). Elsewhere in the visions we notice that the role of Zerubbabel was played down in order to enhance the position of Joshua the high priest (3:1-10; 4:6-10, as submerged within 4:1-5 and 11-14). Once again in 6:9-15 Zerubbabel and the Davidic dynasty are eclipsed as more and more honor is bestowed upon the high priest.

A RELIGIOUS PATH THROUGH A TEXTUAL AND POLITICAL MINEFIELD

The mysterious collapse of the Davidic dynasty (or more specifically, of its representative, the governor Zerubbabel) may be responsible for the many difficulties that plague these verses. As elsewhere in Zechariah, problems surface particularly in texts that deal with Zerubbabel (see the preceding paragraph). Most translations of Zech. 6:9-15 (RSV, JB, NEB, NAB) follow the ancient versions (Greek LXX or Syriac) to smooth over the rough textual spots. In the Hebrew, (1) the names in v. 14 do not completely correspond with those earlier in v. 10; (2) v. 14 begins awkwardly, against the normal Hebrew word order, and has a plural noun/subject connected with a verb in the singular; (3) the final clause in v. 15 dangles in a clumsy way, unfinished. Blotches such as these occur more easily when a text is being transmitted and corrected orally.

The sequence of verses as proposed by David L. Petersen (*Haggai and Zechariah 1–8,* 273) preserves the Hebrew text and fits in

well with another, more conspicuous example of a later insertion
(4:6-10). While 6:9-11 and 14 advance the cause of the high priest
Joshua over that of Zerubbabel, vv. 12-13 center details, even those
concerning the high priest, around Zerubbabel. Verses 12-13 not
only have their own separate and solemn introduction, but they interrupt the discussion of the crowns in the former section. The editor is thus attending to a situation, perhaps existing already in the
lifetime of the prophet Zechariah, in which the Davidic dynasty
made one last bid for its restoration, failed and slipped from the
horizon of governmental office, never again to reappear.

While vv. 12-13 are an oracle of promise and hope for Zerubbabel, the literary form of vv. 9-11, 14 follows the style of symbolic
action on the prophet's part: a sign-oracle, according to Ralph L.
Smith (*Micah—Malachi,* 216-17). A sign is always a real event, but
it is not described for its own sake but rather for a message that it
communicates to contemporary or future generations, such as
Isaiah's walking naked and barefoot (Isa. 20), or Jeremiah's carrying
a wooden yoke across his neck and shoulders (Jer. 28), or the many,
even weird actions of Ezekiel (Ezek. 3:22-27; chs. 4–5). Prophecy
always includes the element of excitement and attention, whether in
the rhetoric of words or in dramatic (even bizarre) actions.

THE FUTURE WITH TEMPLE AND PRIESTHOOD

With gold and silver brought from exile (we almost think of the
Israelites' plundering the Egyptians at the time of their departure
from that country—Exod. 3:19-22; see Peter R. Ackroyd, *Exile and
Restoration,* 195), Zechariah is able to prepare crowns. The Hebrew
reads in the plural in Zech. 6:11 and v. 14. It is possible that Zechariah made two of them, one for Zerubbabel and another for Joshua,
but it is equally possible that the feminine plural form refers to
several bands on a single crown (like the papal tiara, once used for
the inauguration of a new pope) or to a feminine plural ending for
majesty. The word "wisdom" occurs in the feminine plural in Prov.
1:20; 9:1; 14:1 (cf. Job 31:36, "crowns"). If we grant more than a
single crown, the following part of Zech. 6:11 would then read, "Set
[one of them] upon the head of Joshua, son of Jehozadak, the high
priest." The problem remains, however, because the high priest is
not said to wear a *crown* but a *turban* (3:5)! The stickiness of the textual question may reflect political intrigues of any age! Such is the
human situation wherein salvation becomes a reality in flesh and
blood.

Zech. 6:12-13 rather clearly refer to Zerubbabel, for the title of branch or shoot is commonly used of Davidic royalty (see the discussion with 3:8). It seems, moreover, that these verses place Joshua close to Zerubbabel as a peaceful adviser. While harmony seems to exist, the counsel of the adviser can be rejected by the one in charge (cf. 2 Sam. 15:31, 34). "Both explicitly and implicitly the Davidic scion achieves pride of place" (Petersen, 278), but not for long, as we see in the transition to Zech. 6:14, where the crown(s) become(s) the possession of the high priest who places it (them?) in the temple as a memorial offering. First, however, let us note that while most translations differentiate between Zerubbabel *upon his throne* and Joshua *by the throne* (of Zerubbabel), so that Joshua seems subordinate to the king, nonetheless the Hebrew has a single preposition *'al,* so that each may be seated upon his own throne. Perhaps this discussion is nitpicking at the Hebrew, but is that not often the case of politics, nitpicking at legal procedure for one's advantage!

"A memorial in the temple of the LORD" has biblical precedence. We recall the copper image of the snake (Num. 21:9; 2 Kgs. 18:4) and the possibility of Nehemiah's memoirs being a memorial votive offering for the temple (cf. Neh. 13:31, a phrase still used today in synagogues to honor benefactors). We also think of memorial sacrifices in the temple: Exod. 30:16; Num. 10:9-10.

Finally, in Zech. 6:15 Zechariah reaches into the future when Jewish people in the distant Diaspora will continue to support the Jerusalem temple. By silently overlooking the people of the land, rejected by Haggai from participating in the rebuilding of the temple and from its services, Zechariah sees the new people of Israel to consist exclusively of those who have come back from exile. They are the true remnant; the others are contaminated by their pagan neighbors and have not been properly formed in the laws of Moses through the new editing of the Priestly and Deuteronomic traditions of the Torah during the Exile.

Without a doubt, the future of the people Israel lies with the temple and its priesthood, no longer with the Davidic kings. The promises to David are reserved for future fulfillment, possibly beyond the realm of human effort and activity. The Royal Psalms, like Pss. 2 and 110, are reinterpreted of a new Davidic heir to be raised up mysteriously by God. In the meanwhile, Israel approaches God through temple worship.

This insistence upon the temple, at the cost of Davidic royalty and its military forces, reemphasizes what we have seen already. War and rebellion were not the way to go, but rather obedience to the Mosaic law and fervent fulfillment of temple worship. These latter attitudes stabilized Israel for what Yahweh was to do in the future.

THE FINAL PROPHETIC
WARNING AND PROMISE
Zechariah 7:1–8:23

TRUE PROPHECY IN SUMMARY

Chapters 7 and 8 conclude Zechariah's ministry thoroughly on track in customary prophetic style. In fact, one scholar considers 7:7-10 "one of the finest summaries of the teaching of the former prophets" (Ralph L. Smith, *Micah—Malachi*, 225). Typical again of prophecy, a passionate condemnation of social injustice and a stern announcement of its severe punishment occur in ch. 7. This negative side is followed, again as customary with prophecy, by a positive upbeat in ch. 8. Prophecy, especially in its final edited form within the Bible, never ends striking a destructive note. Even a prophetical book as negative as that by Amos closes with joyful singing of "the days [that] are coming":

> when the plowman shall overtake the reaper
> and the treader of grapes him who sows the seed;
> the mountains shall drip sweet wine. . . .
> I will restore the fortunes of my people Israel.
> > (Amos 9:13-14)

This telltale sign of authentic prophecy—an optimistic conclusion that Israel will rise to new life out of the ashes of any destruction—offers us a degree of clarity in distinguishing true from false prophets. As we shall see in discussing ch. 8 of Zechariah, these conclusions to prophetic books generally represent the work of the final editor—certainly someone who knew well the genuine tradition of the prophet, also someone acceptable to the people at large and to the temple personnel and therefore a person of respect and authority. The final acceptance of a prophecy, so important to the overall canonical shape of a book, comes from the central governing body of Israel's religion. Here then is another distinguishing mark of true prophecy: whatever be its challenge and condemnation of Israel's religion, in reality it is not working for the annihilation of religion but for its transformation and worthy continuity into the future.

Prophets, accordingly, remained respondents or reactors to temple priests as well as to Israel's civil leadership, and eventually their "servants." We have already seen in the prophecies of Haggai and Zechariah not only the way by which Zerubbabel and civil authority became absorbed within the role of Joshua and the priesthood but also the way by which prophecy accepts and serves the temple priests. Prophets were not an independent, self-sufficient group like the temple priests. While prophets came and went, Torah and priesthood remained always at the center.

The editor formed a carefully crafted unit of chs. 7–8 and then stitched this finale harmoniously into place. The question about fasting (7:3-5 and 8:18-19) and the role of foreigners (7:1-2 and 8:22-23) constitute an envelope around the other material in the final two chapters. While ch. 7 leads up to the scattering of Israel "with a whirlwind among all the nations" (7:14), ch. 8 closes with "nations of every tongue [taking] hold of the robe of a Jew, saying, 'Let us go with you, for we have heard that God is with you'" (8:23). Typical of many other sections of the OT, Zechariah or his editors do not develop this intuition about the bonding of Israelites and Gentiles in a common worship of the Lord (cf. Amos 9:7; Isa. 19:16-25). It startled people enough simply to state the fact that it will happen.

Not only are chs. 7–8 closely united, but by means of several important ideas they are joined with the opening chapter, where again there is an explicit mention of the "former prophets" (1:4-6; 7:7) and of the "nations" (1:15; 8:22-23). We are not back to where we started, however, for the earth does not remain "at rest" (1:11) nor are the nations "at ease" (1:15). On the contrary, we glimpse intense activity as the inhabitants of many cities are seeking out one another and the nations are streaming towards the new, prosperous Jerusalem (8:20-23). The positive upbeat at the end of Zechariah's prophecy rounds out the entire complex of prophetic preaching and visions. The literary structuring of chs. 1–8 shows that all has been in the steady control of the Lord.

FASTING

The first six verses of ch. 7 raise the question: "Should I mourn and fast in the fifth month, as I have done for so many years?" (v. 3). The source of the question is not clear. The introductory verse can be, and in fact is, rendered differently in various translations and deserves some attention. First, however, all agree upon the reference to "King Darius." Only here and in Hag. 1:1 does he carry the formal title of *king*. Is this a subtle way, as David L. Petersen infers (*Haggai and Zechariah 1–8,* 282), not only to unify the prophecies of Haggai and Zechariah but also to do so with the understanding that this prophecy will be fulfilled without even the presence of a Davidic king, much less his active assistance? The Persian monarch now has exclusive rights to royalty. Israel's aspirations are no longer to center upon kingship and its earthly domain but upon the temple and its priesthood.

"The fourth year of King Darius, . . . the fourth day of the ninth month, which is Chislev," places the event here on 7 December 518 B.C. (Joyce G. Baldwin, *Haggai, Zechariah, Malachi,* 29, 141). Not only the fact that the question is raised four months in advance before the first of the fast days, but also the designation of the month according to the Persian name of Chislev (a practice uncommon till eighty to one hundred years later and to show up only in 1-2 Chronicles), surround this prophetical oracle with distance and later editing. Time allows the question to be pondered seriously and the answer to be edited carefully.

Who sends whom, in v. 2, is open to several variations, even in the ancient versions and manuscripts. We opt for that of Petersen (281): "Bethelsarezer and Regemmelek, and their men, sent to seek help from Yahweh." The names have the ring of Persian nobility (cf. Jer. 39:3 for the use of "sarezer"), so that the delegation of Jews comes from among the exiles in Babylon with the backing of highly placed Persian officials. Accepting the Persian world order, the Jewish people capitalize upon its new peace and benevolence for reviving and improving religious practices. Furthermore, questions about ritual and other legal matters are not to be settled in Babylon but at Jerusalem. Unlike Hag. 2:11, however, the final word at the temple is to be given by prophecy, not by priesthood, perhaps for one of the final times before prophecy becomes completely domesticated within temple ritual, as we see in the books of Joel and Chronicles (cf. 1 Chr. 25:1, where temple singers are called "prophets").

Similar to the way that most biblical legislation developed, a new situation raises questions about older laws and practices. Now that the Exile was officially at an end with the decree of Cyrus in 538 (cf. Ezra 1:1-4) and the temple was rebuilt, the Jews in Babylon questioned whether or not the days of fasting and mourning over the destruction of the holy city and the temple were still obligatory. From Zech. 7:3, 5 and 8:19, we learn that fasting was observed in the following months:

—fourth month, because of the capture of Jerusalem (2 Kgs. 25:2-3; Jer. 39:2)

—fifth month, because of the burning of the temple (2 Kgs. 25:8-9)

—seventh month, because of the assassination of the Jewish governor, Gedaliah (2 Kgs. 25:25; Jer. 41:1-2)

—tenth month, because of the beginning of the siege of Jerusalem (2 Kgs. 25:1).

Fasting, like prophecy, was not only closely linked with historical tragedies but it also had its own history, which we will look at for better appreciating Zechariah's solution.

Through most of Israel's liturgical and legislative history up to the Exile (and in many ways, after the Exile), sickness, suffering, and death—in fact, any diminution of life—were not considered a proper subject for Israel's temple worship. At the end of Noah's flood, God declares that the covenant "is between me and you and every *living* creature of all flesh" (Gen. 9:15). God is the creator and sustainer of life and its good order (Gen. 1), and consequently sickness, disorder, and death do not belong in God's realm nor in the temple. For this reason, priests and especially the high priest were not to contaminate themselves by even touching the dead; and if they were disabled people, they were prohibited from functioning as priests (Lev. 21). In the ritual, moreover, blood did not symbolize death but life (Lev. 17:11; Exod. 24:6-8).

Various liturgical pieces reflect the desperation of people who are mourning their sickness and possible death and have little if any formal ritual for the occasion:

In death there is no remembrance of thee;
in Sheol who can give thee praise.
(Ps 6:5; cf. Isa. 38:18)

When fasting and mourning appear in the early days of Israel, we find the practice not within the legislation of the Torah but within the sphere of popular piety. Penitential acts constituted the people's spontaneous reaction to national disasters or to individual tragedy. After a defeat from the Philistines, the people "gathered at Mizpah, and drew water and poured it out before the LORD, and fasted on that day, and said there, 'We have sinned against the LORD'" (1 Sam. 7:6; cf. Josh. 7:6-9; Judg. 20:6). During the critical sickness of his child, "David fasted, and went in and lay all night upon the ground" (2 Sam. 12:16). These actions, however, find no parallel in the legislation of the Torah.

If fasting is practiced by people in the Torah (except for Lev. 16, which we will discuss below), it was not prompted by sin and sorrow but by holiness and ecstasy. Two examples are each associated with Mt. Sinai or Horeb.

[When Moses] was there with the Lord forty days and forty nights [on Mt. Sinai/Horeb], he neither ate bread nor drank water. And he wrote upon the tables the words of the covenant, the ten commandments. (Exod. 34:28)

Another incident comes from the story of the prophet Elijah. While journeying to Mt. Sinai/Horeb, an angel provided him with "a cake baked on hot stones and a jar of water" (1 Kgs. 19:6). After eating, he "went in the strength of that food [and therefore fasting] forty days and forty nights to Horeb the mount of God" (v. 8). An ecstatic experience followed with the vision of Yahweh in "a still small voice" (v. 12).

During the Exile fasting at first was probably unnecessary; few if any of the people had enough food for adequate nourishment, much less excess food to put aside in a gesture of fasting and penance. Life itself was more than enough of a penance. However, as days began to distance the people from the destruction of Jerusalem and its magnificent temple, various forms of self-denial and mourning were introduced lest these tragedies be forgotten. Fasting, in this case, is a ritual for remembering and reliving tragic days; it is a way of seeking the Lord's merciful care in the event of new disasters. Fasting also was recognized as a bonding with destitute or sorrowful people, so that these can share their great dependence upon God with others better off than themselves and in danger of forgetting God in their abundance.

Some type of liturgical mourning for sin and of seeking at-one-ment with God within the community began to emerge during the Exile. In Ezek. 45:18-20 the Hebrew text places this ceremony of purifying the sanctuary on the first day of the first month and again on the seventh day of the month; the latter day is changed to the first day of the seventh month in the Greek version (followed by the NAB), while Neh. 9:1 stipulates that "on the twenty-fourth day of this [seventh] month" the leaders gathered together fasting and in sackcloth. It is possible that eventually all of these various traditions about fasting were united on one all-holy day, now called Yom Kippur, to be placed "in the seventh month, on the tenth day" (Lev. 16:29). Yet in the ritual for Yom Kippur fasting is not explicitly mentioned, only that "you shall afflict yourselves, and shall do no work." If Lev. 16 were to have existed from the Mosaic age, it is difficult to understand all the questions about fasting during the Exile and immediately afterwards. In fact, there is total silence about it elsewhere in the Torah and in preexilic prophecy.

As we gauge from the fast days mentioned in Zech. 7–8, the penitential acts are not associated with events in early Israelite history but rather with tragedies at the time of the destruction of Jerusalem and the temple. Fasting, accordingly, moved from the arena of popular piety (non-Torah, non-temple oriented) into the official religion of Israel by force of the circumstances of later Israelite history. Once these horrendous deeds were associated with the expressed will of God and this prophetic judgment accepted by the people and their religious leaders, then fasting could be officially sanctioned and even ordered. The practice becomes very evident in the book of Joel:

> Sanctify a fast,
>> call a solemn assembly.
> Gather the elders
>> and all the inhabitants of the land
> to the house of the LORD your God;
>> and cry to the LORD.
> Alas for the day!
> For the day of the LORD is near.
>> (Joel 1:14-15)

The setting is "secular," a devastating locust plague, considered religiously to be a "day of the LORD." As we observe this prophetic theme of "the day of the LORD" from Amos 5:18 and especially from Zeph. 1:14-16 to Joel (who quotes from Zephaniah), we observe a transformation from military invasion to locust plague, from the arena of politics and agriculture into the sacred area of the temple.

With the Exile over and with Haggai's announcement that the promised final age was at hand (cf. Hag. 2:6-9), the people had questions about observing the days of fasting. In addressing the question, Zechariah follows the normal response of prophecy to any religious activity: look to the motives that inspire persons to act as they do. The early postexilic prophet Trito- or Third Isaiah called for a day of fasting in which one looses the bonds of wickedness from oneself and the yoke of oppression from the poor, by bringing the homeless into one's own house and sharing bread with the hungry. Trito-Isaiah concludes with striking prophetical rhetoric: Thus you will not "hide yourself from your own flesh" (Isa. 58:6-7). This is "a fast, and a day acceptable to the LORD" (Isa. 58:5). In commenting upon this passage, George A. F. Knight links it with the time even before Haggai and Zechariah. Wealthy people among the civil and religious leaders were cheating "those unskilled labourers [who] were probably being employed now to build [their] homes . . . In a word, then, the fast of hypocrites is an abomination to the Lord. True fasting must be motivated by repentance and love" (*The New Israel,* 25).

Zechariah's response is a model sermon, as noted by Rex A. Mason ("Some Echoes of the Preaching in the Second Temple?" *ZAW* 96 [1984]: 221-235). We find: (1) an appeal to all the people, not just to kings, prophets or priests; (2) an appeal to accepted authority, the "former prophets" and indirectly to the Torah in insisting upon kindness and justice (Exod. 34:6-7); (3) theological teaching about God; (4) prophetic warnings, here about the wrath of God against perpetrators of injustice; (5) questions that appeal for an answer from the audience and other rhetorical means to hold attention. The words move in and out of poetic meter, so that prose intercepts the poetic momentum and seriously fixes the attention of the audience.

We hear many echoes of prophetic preaching:

—caring for the widow and orphan (Isa. 1:17, 23);

—stubbornness (Hos. 4:16);

—ears too heavy to hear (Isa. 6:10);

—heart as hard as diamonds (Jer. 17:1; Ezek. 3:9);

—outburst of God's wrath (Jer. 15:14);

—storm wind of divine anger (Hab. 3:14).

Zechariah is touching all the keys of the organ, so that each idea or sound brings back memories of prophets who threatened Jerusalem with destruction. This is no idle threat, for it had come true. For the future the solution lies in such simple human virtues as caring for one's own flesh and blood as typified in the orphan and the widow. Not only the history of Jerusalem and the Jewish people, but world history as well depends upon the basic reaction of compassion and concern for the needy.

A REFLECTION FROM THE
DISCIPLES OF ZECHARIAH
Zechariah 8:1-23

Because prophecy was principally the *living* word of God *preached* and *heard*, it continued to live not just by being inscribed on parchment but also by being continuously preached to new generations. Chapter 8 seems one of those latter examples, as found already in the book of Jeremiah (compare the later sermon of Jer. 7 with its earlier inspiration in Jer. 26), in which passages are drawn from the memory of Zechariah's preaching as well as from other prophetic sources. Zechariah 8:9 seems to refer to such a situation: "you who in these days have been hearing these words from the mouth of the prophets," not just of Zechariah but of others too. Chapters 1 and 7 had already referred similarly to the "former prophets" (1:4, 6; 7:7, 12), as though they (with Zechariah) are no longer alive or at least not present with the congregation.

A dynamic interchange of preaching and listening rings out with such phrases as: "Jerusalem shall be *called* the faithful city" (8:3); those "who in these days *have been hearing* these words from the mouth of the prophets" (v. 9); or again, "*speak* the truth to one another" (v. 16).

A book of the prophet, therefore, represents more than an inspired text from an inspired individual; it also comes to us from an inspired tradition, which lived from the earlier word of God but also adapted it so as to direct and sanctify new circumstances. Speaking more specifically, we see just such a need of adaptation in the question of fasting: are the four great fasts still binding? Prophecy, more so than Torah and priesthood, was particularly gifted with the ability to challenge old laws (of inspired origin, indeed) that were no longer serving their earlier exalted purpose. It was to prophecy that people turned for the answer, not just to a renowned individual like Zechariah but also to his disciples of the next generation, as we saw happening in 7:4, 8.

The sermon or sermons in ch. 8 divide clearly enough into ten very short oracles, beginning with vv. 1, 3, 4, 6, 7, 9, 14, 18, 20, 23. The number "ten," though sanctified by the decalogue of Moses, may simply mean a complete or full rounding of what God wants. The oft repeated introduction, "Thus says the LORD of hosts," enables the preacher to rise in crescendo to an ever more emphatic statement at the end. The longest section, vv. 9-13, may represent a separate sermon; it begins and ends with the identical phrase, "let your hands be strong." This literary device is called "inclusion" and is frequently used to circumscribe the limits of a sermon, poem, or narrative. Verses 9-13 carry the trademarks of a temple sermon, as already found in ch. 7 and elsewhere in the book of Chronicles (cf. 2 Chr. 15:3-7).

ON PILGRIMAGE TO GOD
IN THE JERUSALEM TEMPLE

Although, as we will show, Jerusalem occupies the most prominent place in this concluding chapter, it may be said that the invisible God of the temple is still more central. The concluding words of Zech. 8 state simply one of the principal goals of prophecy vis à vis the temple, "We have heard that God is with you" (8:23). What Isaiah addressed to the Davidic dynasty more than two hundred years earlier at Jerusalem, "*Immanu-el*—With us [is] God" (Isa. 7:14; 8:8, 10; cf. Ps. 46:7, 11), resounds in the final phrase of ch. 8 of Zechariah: "*elohim immakem*—God [is] with you." Another important verse in Zechariah highlights the necessity of seeking God, not ritual ceremony, in the temple:

> The inhabitants of one city shall go to another, saying, "Let us go at once to entreat the favor of the LORD, and to seek the LORD of hosts; I am going." (v. 21)

The final phrase, "I am going," reads with exceptional, personal emphasis in the Hebrew text: "*I am going,* indeed I myself." The desire for personal bonding with God in the holy temple became all consuming.

Yahweh's presence at the temple, real but invisible, depends upon the faith of Israel, which reaches out towards the poor and needy in their midst and which recognizes how equally poor and needy is every Israelite. It is not that human faith produces the divine presence, for God is already awaiting the Israelites who are on pilgrimage to the temple, a theme insistently present in the long prayer of Solomon (1 Kgs. 8:15-53 as well as in the Songs of Ascent (Pss. 120–134).

THE LORD'S ENTHRONEMENT

The temple on earth reflects a divine enthronement above the heavens, as Solomon declared:

> But will God indeed dwell on the earth? Behold, heaven and the highest heaven cannot contain thee; how much less this house which I have built! (1 Kgs. 8:27)

The psalms frequently enough look to the primary, eternal home of God, splendidly above this earth:

> The LORD sits enthroned over the flood;
> the LORD sits enthroned as king for ever.
> (Ps. 29:10)

Psalm 150, moreover, moves the focus from God's heavenly home to God's redemptive acts in Israel's history, from the celebration of these great deeds in temple ritual to a festivity across the entire earth:

> *God's heavenly home:*
>   Praise God in his sanctuary;
>   praise him in his mighty firmament!
> *God's mighty acts in Israel's history:*
>   Praise him for his mighty deeds;
>   praise him according to his exceeding greatness!
> *God's earthly home and its ritual:*
>   Praise him with trumpet sound . . . with lute and harp!
>   . . . with strings and pipe! . . . with loud clashing cymbals!
> *Praise across the universe:*
>   Let everything that breathes praise the LORD!

God is free to move from one "temple" of divine presence to another. Yahweh's enthronement in the Jerusalem temple is conditioned, by divine will, upon Israel's fidelity to the Covenant. The Lord abandoned the temple because of Israel's wickedness (cf. Ezek. 10:18-19; 11:22-25) and returned because of divine mercy (cf. Ezek. 43:1-5). Haggai announced that this promise was fulfilled in the new temple (Hag. 2:6-9). Zechariah 8:3 reaffirms Haggai's statement:

> Thus says the LORD: I will return to Zion, and will dwell in the midst of Jerusalem, and Jerusalem shall be called the faithful city, and the mountain of the LORD of hosts, the holy mountain.

These words of Zechariah echo Isaiah's prophecy about the faithful city (Isa. 1:26) as well as the temple tradition about the mountain of the Lord (Ps. 48).

JEALOUS FOR THE POOR AND NEEDY

Fidelity on Israel's part is expressed by way of sympathy for the poor and needy. Zechariah draws a sketch of: (1) old men and old women, sitting in the streets of Jerusalem, each with staff in hand because of old age; (2) streets full of boys and girls at play (Zech. 8:4). As Theodore Cuyler Speers remarked: we should "measure the significance of our cities by their effect upon two groups easily overlooked—the old and the young" (*IB* 6:1085). Jerusalem's worldwide centrality, as mentioned in the commentary upon ch. 7, is closely—indeed, inextricably—related to care and security for the young and the elderly.

Understandably, the preceding oracle in Zech. 8 reiterates the *jealousy* of the Lord. Wherever there is tender and intimate love, always the case in a family that cares for its elderly and welcomes its children, jealous watchfulness prevails. People are on guard against marauders from outside and against insidious betrayals from inside the family circle:

> I am jealous for Zion with great jealousy, and I am jealous for her with great wrath. (8:2)

The Hebrew sound rings with booming repetition:

> *qinne'ti letsiyyon qin'ah gedolah*
> *wehemah gedolah qinne'ti lah.*

Jacques Guillet wrote in the *Dictionary of Biblical Theology:*

> The jealous zeal of God is another aspect of His interior intensity. It is the passion that He brings to all He does and to all that He touches. . . . When the prophets discover that this passion of God for the work of His hands is the passion of a spouse, the theme takes on a new intensity and intimacy. The divine jealousy is at one and the same time a fearful wrath and a vulnerable tenderness. (207)

In continuity with this blending of tenderness and wrath within the notion of jealousy, we find that the word "wrath" is one of the means by which Zechariah or his disciples stitch together chs. 7 and 8 (7:12; 8:2, 14).

A MORE UNIVERSAL CALL

At the same time the prophet does not allow this jealous concern and simmering wrath to inhibit him from opening wide the city gates to people even from other nations. First he calls upon Israelites who had been scattered at the time of the Exile, had gradually sunk roots in foreign soil, and had become known as the Diaspora. Zechariah hears God address them:

> I will save my people from the east country and from the west country; and I will bring them to dwell in the midst of Jerusalem; and they shall be my people and I will be their God, in faithfulness and in righteousness. (8:7-8)

Again many prophetical passages come to mind in hearing this address:

> "I will bring them from the north country, and . . . from the farthest parts of the earth, among them the blind and the lame." (Jer. 31:7-8)

> "They shall be my people, and I will be their God." (Ezek. 37:23, and frequently in the Bible)

> "Afterward you shall be called the city of righteousness, the faithful city." (Isa. 1:26)

Zechariah considers the pilgrimage from the Diaspora to Jerusalem to be important for salvation (Zech. 8:7-8). Their pilgrimage externalizes what God is already doing internally in their midst as the chosen people: "I will bring them." Their dwelling in Jerusalem is proposed as a sacred way of living, even a ritual of worship. In the phrase, "I will bring them *to dwell*," Zechariah uses a Hebrew word, *shakan*, with a long history from secular usage to a sacred meaning. *Shakan* originally referred to living in tents during nomadic or semi-nomadic times and was then transferred to the "meeting tent" where Yahweh dwelt with the people (Exod. 40:2). The noun, *mishkan*, refers to Yahweh's dwelling place, the Jerusalem temple. Here Israel prayed that divine "glory *may dwell* in our land" (Ps. 85:9) and "Jerusalem *will dwell* securely [and its name shall be] 'The Lord is our righteousness'" (Jer. 33:16).

Not only fellow Jews will stream towards Jerusalem, but "ten men from the nations of every tongue shall take hold of the robe of a Jew, saying, 'Let us go with you, for we have heard that God is with you'" (Zech. 8:23). What was an emphatic statement by the

Jewish person in v. 21, "*I am going,* indeed, I myself (author's translation)," is now repeated by the Gentiles, "*Let us go.*"

At first it may seem strange, even contradictory that foreigners are invited but the local people of the land, who had never gone into exile are rejected as unclean (see the Introduction to Haggai and Zechariah; also the commentary on Hag. 2:10-13). Zechariah 8:10 refers to the opposition from this group in the rebuilding of the temple. Only "the remnant of this people [those who had returned from exile are] to possess all these things" (vv. 10-12). Yet as far back as Gen. 10 in the Table of Nations, those people who lived closest to the Israelites (called the children of Ham) were the ones to be feared the most, while those who were safely at a distance (called the children of Japheth) could be dealt with more benevolently. In the postexilic age, now that the Jewish people had given up the idea of an impressive civil and military presence on the world scene, empires like those of the Persians no longer posed a serious threat, but people close by who were half-Jew and half-Gentile, half observant and half nonobservant of the law in its new, postexilic interpretations, these were the ones to be feared, avoided, and even repudiated. Here is the dark side of jealousy and intimate love.

The prophetic vision of the new Jerusalem may seem like fanciful daydreaming. To that the prophet and the temple preacher reply:

> If it is marvelous [a better translation is "too marvelous" or, as in the NAB, "impossible"] in the sight of the remnant of this people in these days, should it also be [too] marvelous in my sight, says the LORD of hosts? (v. 6)

To the later generation, afraid that they will never see the wonders announced by Haggai, the disciples of Zechariah reiterate their faith in the future glory of the temple at Jerusalem. They also repeat the prophetic expectation of kindliness towards the needy (here the elderly and the children, vv. 4-5) and of honesty and good thoughts in all transactions, whether publicly at the city gate or more privately between individual families (vv. 16-17). Then fasting will be turned back into "seasons of joy and gladness, and cheerful feasts [with] truth and peace" (v. 19). Fasting then will not be an occasion of mourning over sin and disaster but an attitude of the pure, undistracted person, who like Moses and Elijah approaches the mysterious presence of God within the temple.

12-21-94

THE PROPHECY OF
SECOND ZECHARIAH,
CHS. 9–14

INTRODUCTION

We enter into one of the most obscure sections of the Bible, where the Hebrew text is often enough in damaged condition and where historical data, conveniently provided for us in the first part of Zechariah (chs. 1–8), is suddenly and completely missing. Yet we are also privileged to explore that part of the Hebrew Scriptures most quoted in the Gospel narrative pertaining to the passion, death, and resurrection of Jesus and frequently enough called upon in the early preaching of the Church.

RELATION WITH FIRST ZECHARIAH

As we shall see, the differences between chs. 1–8 and 9–14 are rather significant, yet at the same time there are many points of contact. We are dealing with different authors at different times of Israel's history, yet we recognize family resemblances. The differences show up clearly enough in the following schema:

	Zech. 1–8	Zech. 9–14
Date	Oct./Nov. 520 to Nov. 518	No dates are provided
History	Zerubbabel, Joshua, Darius	No mention of any person by name
	Temple Reconstruction	No explicit mention of temple
Author	Zechariah by name	Anonymous; only 11:4-17 in first person
Style	Prose; involved, redundant; visionary	Poetic; more apocalyptic; no visions
Atmosphere	More peaceful and secure	More militaristic and uncertain
Religious leaders	Respected	Found unworthy

113

| *Davidic dynasty* | Quietly disappears | Mourned; peaceful revival expected |
| *Messianic hopes* | Especially under the priesthood | Especially under Yahweh as King |

These differences, especially of a topical or religious nature, are further developed by Rex A. Mason, "The Relation of Zech 9–14 to Proto-Zechariah," *ZAW* 88 (1976): 227-239.

At the same time many points of contact show up, so that we can trace family resemblances in this inspired tradition. Brevard S. Childs (*Introduction to the Old Testament as Scripture*, 482-83) points out several parallels between chs. 1–8 and chs. 9–14:

1. a new Jerusalem without walls (2:5; 9:8; 14:11);
2. the return of paradisal fertility (8:12; 14:6, 8);
3. ancient covenant promise (8:8; 13:9);
4. curse in 5:3 is reversed in 14:11;
5. a divine judgment against the nations (1:18-21; 14:12) and conversion of the nations to Yahweh (2:11; 8:20, 22; 14:16);
6. ingathering of the exiles (8:7; 10:9-10);
7. new cultic rites for the new age (8:18-19; 14:16-21);
8. outpouring of the Spirit, cleansing (4:6; 12:10) and transforming (5:4; 13:3);
9. a humble messianic figure (3:8; 4:6; 9:9-10).

OTHER BONDINGS IN ZECHARIAH 9–14

At the beginning of chs. 9 and 12 and again at the beginning of ch. 1 of Malachi, the editor appended a special introductory word (Hebrew *massa'*), which is variously translated as "oracle," "burden," or "pronouncement" (see Zech. 9:1). A new beginning is seen at ch. 12, not only with the presence of *massa'* but also with the inclusion of a few lines of a hymn, frequently enough a way of introducing a prophetic book (cf. Amos 1:2; Mic. 1:2-4; Isa. 2:2-5). Along with the new introduction at Zech. 12:1, other differences separate chs. 12–14 from chs. 9–11. The concern of the author in chs. 12–14 reaches out favorably beyond Jerusalem to the clans of Judah rather than being focused exclusively upon Jerusalem. While disillusion spreads its dullness over the final section of chs. 9–11, this attitude modulates into mourning in ch. 12 and ends with the Lord's royal, messianic triumph in ch. 14. While we do find hopes for a new beginning in chs. 9–11, these are more humble and certainly less dramatic than the final pilgrimage of the world to Jerusalem in ch.

14. It is difficult to know if these differences are indicative of separate, inspired authors or of the same author over a long stretch of time.

Throughout the commentary we will be citing the many references to other prophets in chs. 9–14. This tendency was already seen in chs. 1–8, especially with the references to "the former prophets" (1:4-5; 7:7, 12), but the contact with other prophetical books now becomes so frequent that Rex A. Mason remarks: "To some extent the prophet of the living word is giving way to the exegete of the written word" (*The Books of Haggai, Zechariah and Malachi*, 80). The many examples of borrowing from earlier prophets have been studied by Matthias Delcor, "Les sources du Deutéro-Zacharie et ses procédés d'emprunt," *RB* 59 (1952): 385-411.

Delcor cites particularly the tendency to borrow from Ezekiel, then from Second and Third Isaiah and Jeremiah, and to a more limited yet significant degree from Zephaniah, Deuteronomy, and Joel. For instance, the statement "half to the east and half to the west" is found only in Joel 2:20 and Zech. 14:8. Yet there are profound differences between Second Zechariah and Joel, especially in the former's willingness to admit foreigners to the temple (Zech. 14:16) in stern contrast to the latter's summons to a holy war against the nations (Joel 3:9-10). In this regard, it is interesting to note that Second Zechariah is more open towards the nations than Joel but not as expansive as Third Isaiah, who even sees some of the foreigners being taken "for priests and for Levites" (Isa. 66:21). Evidently despite the abundant borrowing Second Zechariah pursued related, but separate theological aims.

ADVANCES TOWARD ESCHATOLOGICAL AND APOCALYPTIC FORMS

The characteristics of apocalyptic literature are discussed with ch. 14: i.e., its extravagant use of symbols, the reliance upon ancient personages and literature to draw up an account of what is about to happen, its sense of the end of one age and the dawning of the final age of the world, the titanic battle between good and evil forces, the collapse of all human powers before the almighty presence of Yahweh. As we compare these qualities of apocalyptic literature with the style of ch. 14, we note some serious differences, as pointed out in the commentary. If, for instance, some of the nations refuse to come up to Jerusalem and are punished with lack of rain or other types of scourges (14:17-19), then the absolute victory of goodness over evil has not yet been achieved.

Comparing Zech. 9–14 with Isa. 24–27 and especially with Dan. 7–12, we realize that Second Zechariah remains less certain or less final than these latter authors in placing the final age of the world before us. The "Apocalypse of Isaiah" presents it in this definitive way:

> On this mountain the LORD of hosts will make for all peoples a feast of fat things. . . . He will destroy on this mountain the covering that is cast over all peoples, the veil that is spread over all nations. He will swallow up death for ever, and the LORD GOD will wipe away tears from all faces, and the reproach of his people he will take away from all the earth, for the LORD has spoken. (Isa. 25:6-8)

Still other aspects of Zech. 9–14, or even 12–14 lead us to be cautious about attributing full apocalyptic style to the chapters, like the presence of evil shepherds and the mourning over the beloved. The Lord's final victory of joy and goodness is still not fully at hand.

There are other uncertainties or ambiguities about these chapters that argue against full apocalyptic style. At times the nations are being punished (12:2-4; 14:2, 12-15, 17-19); at other times there is a more gracious openness to them (9:1-8). While most of the book of Zechariah is indifferent or hostile towards the local people who had not gone into exile but were left behind at that time, yet in a few passages such as 11:7; 12:6-8 they seem to be preferred over the people of Jerusalem. The size of the promised land appears very extensive in 10:10 but is quite reduced in the final chapter (14:10).

In this discussion of the rise of eschatological and apocalyptic styles in Zech. 9–14, we also note the demise of prophecy as we have known it up till now. While First Zechariah reinstated prophecy as a champion of social justice more emphatically than what we read in Haggai (Zech. 5:1-4; 7:8-14), Second Zechariah had to admit that prophecy has fallen into the same devious, venal ways of other corrupt forms of religious leadership (13:2-6).

In this ambiguity, which places Second Zechariah somewhere between the end of a former age and the beginning of the final age, we ought to find ourselves at home theologically and spiritually. As Christians we live in the final age of the world, and yet we are still awaiting the second coming of the Lord Jesus. Just when and how Jesus will appear again is not clear to us, despite the benefit of the NT Scriptures.

DATE

As might be suspected, it is very difficult to arrive at a definite date for the composition or even the editing of these chapters. If the portrait of the end of the world is more advanced in Isa. 24–27, that does not necessarily mean that the Isaian passage had to come later. Some leaders live far ahead of their times intellectually or spiritually; others live later but do not share the same advanced theology.

Some of the closest parallels to Zech. 9–14 are located in Isa. 56:9–57:13 and Ps. 16. Here we encounter unfaithful religious leaders, discouragement, and a hope that leaps over all these obstacles. These passages locate us somewhere before the religious reform of Ezra in 428 B.C. We may arrive at a proximate date around 470-460, yet even this location of Second Zechariah is open to question. Who is to say that a religious decline among Israel's leaders never again occurred in Judaism after Ezra!

It is not necessary to place Zech. 9–14 after the conquest of Alexander the Great in 333 and the establishment of the Greek kingdoms in Egypt and Antioch. Neither the reference in Zech. 9:13 to *yawan* (a Hebrew word for Greece) nor the route of the invasion in 9:1-8 proves such a date. Some translators, including the NAB, bracket 9:13 as a later, editorial addition. The word can also simply refer to Greek colonists along the coast of Asia Minor, a situation that reaches back very early. The poem in 9:1-8 has too many biblical antecedents to finalize the date of Zechariah.

A statement of Ralph L. Smith summarizes the question of date quite well: "Chaps. 9–14 probably were produced in Palestine by a disciple of Zechariah at the end of the sixth or at the beginning of the fifth century B.C." (*Micah—Malachi,* 170).

ZECHARIAH 9–14 AND THE NEW TESTAMENT

These chapters of Zechariah constituted a rich mine for NT writers, especially in the narrative of the passion, death, and resurrection of Jesus. C. H. Dodd lines up these citations (*According to the Scriptures,* 64-67):

Zech. 9:9	Matt. 21:5; John 12:15
Zech. 11:13	Matt. 27:9
Zech. 12:3	Luke 21:24
Zech. 12:10	John 19:37; Rev. 1:7
Zech. 13:7	Mark 14:27

The following parallels are also brought to our attention:

Zech. 14:5   1 Thess. 3:13
Zech. 14:8   John 7:38
Zech. 14:21   John 2:16

Further study of these citations and parallels has been done by F. F. Bruce, *New Testament Development of Old Testament Themes*. In the final chapter on "The Shepherd King," Bruce compares the NT with Qumran use of seven passages from Zechariah and comes to some helpful conclusions. Both the NT and Qumran interpret earlier passages in the light of their own situation; both reinterpret in terms of their own leader, be this person the Teacher of Righteousness or Jesus. Both selected the OT passage that best described or expressed their own unique theology (see Zech. 12:10 below). The NT especially advances the role of the Gentiles in the kingdom of God.

This process of reinterpretation has already been seen within the OT use of earlier passages. Zechariah 9–14 did not remain within the setting or even the precise theological stance of Joel or Isa. 24–27, but advanced or restricted the role of the nations. Just as we have witnessed a continuing, inspired tradition within the prophecies of Haggai and Zechariah, the same ongoing development extends the line from these two prophets into the NT. The later passage generally expands the focus of the earlier one. We turn to the older passage, not so much to prove a position of the NT but rather to get to its depth of meaning.

The question of NT interpretation is discussed further in connection with 11:4-7; 12:10-14; 13:7-9.

DIVISION AND DEVELOPMENT

We cite only the larger divisions; for the breakdown into smaller sections, see the commentary.

9:1–11:3   God's Holy War and Jerusalem's Ultimate Peace
11:4-17   Shepherd and Flock: What Each Deserves
12:1–13:6   The New Covenant Through Victory Over the
            Nations, Cleansing, and Mourning
13:7-9   Martyrdom, Renewal, and Remnant
14:1-21   The Finale: Apocalyptic and Cultic

GOD'S HOLY WAR AND JERUSALEM'S ULTIMATE PEACE

Zechariah 9:1–11:3

The division of material within chs. 9–14 is admittedly very difficult. As mentioned in the introduction to this section, no explanation draws a scholarly consensus. In scanning the chapters one's attention is drawn to the poetic meter of 9:1–11:3, and one thinks of the possibility of treating them as a unit thematically. We find not only an interaction of words and ideas but also an "inclusion" that unites the beginning (9:1-8) and the end (11:1-3) with the Lord's victory in the territory around Israel. This area was once included in the boundaries of the promised land. The following sequence may guide us in reflecting upon these chapters of Zechariah:

9:1-8   The full range of the promised land where Yahweh rests as in a temple of divine presence;

9:9-10   The messianic king in a liturgical procession arrives at Jerusalem; (coming of the king)

9:11-17   God, as a warrior, through serious conflict brings peace to Jerusalem;

10:1-2   Prophetic warning against superstition;

10:3-12   Yahweh's holy war (as in 9:11-17) and the return from exile;

11:1-3   A taunt song over the fall of Israel's enemies across the promised land.

THE FULL RANGE
OF THE PROMISED LAND
Zechariah 9:1-8

The first part, in which Yahweh is spoken about in the third person, severely condemns the nations of Philistia, Tyre-Sidon, and Damascus (9:1-6a); then the style and tone change abruptly, with Yahweh's speaking in his own name in the first person singular and announcing the conversion of the Philistines and of the Jebusites, the former inhabitants of Jerusalem. All this is entitled either a Proclamation, or a Burden, or an Oracle, depending on one's translation of Hebrew *massa'*. The root of this word designates something to be carried, consequently something of serious personal concern and so something that weighs heavily upon the soul. In fact, *massa'* will occur two more times, introducing, as it does, chs. 9–11, 12–14, and Mal. 1:1. As mentioned already, this is one of the many ways by which chs. 9–14 are separated from the preceding section of this prophecy.

What is still more pronounced about chs. 9–14 and shows up at once in this opening poem, is the greater reliance upon sacred Scripture. The preaching of the "former prophets," as already mentioned with Zech. 1:4; 7:7, 12; 8:9, is now enshrined in written, authoritative scrolls. Prophets of this new generation certainly consider themselves in a living, inspired continuity with the former ones (otherwise, why would they or the inspired editors at the temple have attached their own words to the scrolls of the masters?), yet they invoke the words of the former in a way that the former did not do of their own predecessors.

Any number of foreign military forces have swept down upon Israel from the north, ranging from the massive campaigns of the dreaded armies of Assyria and Babylon, to the incursions from the city-state of Damascus. Zechariah 9:1-8, however, reverses the process. This time the conquest of the Philistine cities as well as of Tyre and Sidon and of Damascus enable the borders of Israel to reach outward to their largest extent since King David's time. This wide boundary of territory for the promised land is seen in quite a number of biblical texts: Num. 13:21-24; 34:1-12; Deut. 1:7; Josh.

1:3-4; 1 Kgs. 8:65; 2 Kgs. 14:25, 28; Ezek. 47:16. A more limited stretch of territory is envisaged in the stereotyped phrase, "from Dan to Beersheba" (Judg. 20:1; 1 Sam. 3:20; 2 Sam. 17:11, etc.); this latter corresponds more closely to the present state of Israel.

Yet, the purpose in this section of Zechariah is not primarily military, not even geographical, but rather symbolical. People whom even Deuteronomy considered beyond the pale of election as God's chosen ones, are accepted within the ranks of Israel, even "a mongrel people . . . in Ashdod." Deuteronomy 23:2 uses the identical Hebrew word for people of mixed blood who are to be rejected "even to the tenth generation." Moreover, these same unfortunate persons were excluded in Neh. 13:23-25. The disciples of Zechariah foresee a new kind of universalism. The word "remnant," which had been reserved for the returnees from exile in the first part of Zechariah (Zech. 8:12), is now applied to foreigners (9:7).

Zechariah 9:1-8 not only takes a much broader view of "chosen people" than Deut. 23, Haggai, and Zech. 1–8, but this section of the prophecy is also vigorously reworking several prophetic texts about foreigners. It does include a restatement of destruction of fire upon Philistine cities from the oracles against the nations in Amos 1:4, 7, 10, 12, 14; but Amos' announcement of "exile beyond Damascus" is now overturned. The territory of Israel reaches upward to include Damascus, and the earlier prophecy in 2 Kgs. 14:24-27 about Israel's boundaries being restored "from the entrance to Hamath as far as the Sea of the Arabah" is realized. Again, the view here is not military conquest but a spiritual bonding with Gentiles, left vague and undeveloped.

The text highlights the religious aspects of the new chosen people. They are not to eat unclean food (Zech. 9:7; Lev. 11:2-23); selfish hopes are to be banished (Zech. 9:6b); pride and luxury have no place (vv. 2-4).

Peace is to be achieved through the presence of Yahweh, who will "rest" or "encamp at my house as a guard" (v. 8). There is possibly an allusion here to the eighth vision of Zechariah: "Those [horsemen] who go toward the north country have set my Spirit *at rest* in the north country" (6:8). The phrase in 9:8, "at my house," may refer to the temple, but since this sacred building is not otherwise explicitly mentioned in Zech. 9–14, it is possible that the reference here is simply to the *land* where all Israel forms a liturgical community (cf. Jer. 12:7, "I have forsaken *my house,* I have abandoned *my heritage*").

Again as in Zech. 8, so here too the focus is upon the person of

Yahweh: first of all at the beginning of 9:8, where "I will encamp at my house," and then at the very end of the verse, "for now I see with *my own* eyes *('enay).*" This final phrase has been treated quite differently by various scholars and translators: The NEB puts brackets around it and considers it a much later addition; the NAB emends the Hebrew to read, "I have regard for their affliction *('onyo)*." Some will interpret the Hebrew to be the editor's reflection: I myself have seen the fulfillment. Preserving the Hebrew, we read an excellent conclusion to the opening poem for the poetic unit, 9:1–11:3.

THE MESSIANIC KING'S ARRIVAL AT JERUSALEM

Zechariah 9:9-10

The king comes to Jerusalem amid the grandeur and sacredness of a liturgical procession. While this short poem rings with joy from the Lord's people Israel, the concluding section (11:1-3) of this larger poetic unit is marked with cultic expressions of sorrow from Israel's enemies. The liturgical style indicates what will become ever more evident in this series of poems, that the acquisition of the promised land and of complete peace will not be due to any military force on Israel's part but exclusively to the Lord's might and determination. Comparison of this entry of the Davidic king into Jerusalem with David's entry after the revolt of Absalom (2 Sam. 19) reveals literary parallels, yet there is also the essential difference: the Lord alone wages this holy war.

While the prophet speaks in Zech. 9:9, announcing the liturgical procession, the Lord speaks in v. 10, proclaiming the end of conflict and the institution of peace for the messianic king. The language of the opening two lines is intensely liturgical.

A clear liturgical note is sounded with the opening call to "Rejoice!" This word (Hebrew *gil*) is frequently used with other words that mean to cry aloud, exult, break forth in joy. It indicates "an act of expressing joy in spontaneous, enthusiastic cries," generally "without spoken and sung words" (Christoph Barth, "gyl," *TDOT* 2: 471, 473). There is a high frequency of this word in prophecy and psalms, implying joyful expectation breaking beyond human limitations into ecstasy and divine fulfillment: e.g., Ps. 96:11-13:

> Let the heavens be glad, and let the earth *rejoice;*
>> let the sea roar, and all that fills it;
>> let the field exult, and everything in it!
> Then shall all the trees of the wood sing for joy
>> before the Lord, for he comes,
>> for he comes to judge the earth.

A second, highly liturgical word occurs in Zech. 9:9. "Shout aloud" (Hebrew *rua*ʿ) is associated with royal coronations (1 Sam.

10:24), with war cries (Josh. 6:10, 16, 20), and with moments of great rejoicing in the temple (Ps. 47:1; 66:1; 81:1, etc.). Both this word and the preceding one bring memories of temple celebrations, honoring Yahweh with enthusiasm that reaches beyond words.

The one who is called upon to rejoice and shout is "daughter of Zion . . . daughter of Jerusalem!" The holy city is considered here in the feminine gender, as cities are elsewhere in the Bible. The walled city that engenders and protects life is being compared to a pregnant woman (cf. Isa. 54).

In the second part of Zech. 9:9 the Hebrew language makes it evident that the king whose entrance is surrounded with ecstatic joy: (1) finds the fulfillment of messianic promises in his own person; (2) experiences the Lord's saving activity in himself; and (3) is a person of peace.

Many messianic prophecies crowd into mind, among them Isa. 9:1-7 in which the Lord engages in the holy war to roll back darkness from the northern part of the country and to await the child whose name shall be, "Wonderful Counselor, Mighty God, Everlasting Father, Prince of Peace." Even if this poem was originally composed for the coronation of King Hezekiah, as were Pss. 2 and 110 for other kings, nonetheless, with the eclipse of the Davidic dynasty during the Exile and early postexilic period, all of these texts took on a new messianic aura and supported the people's faith in the mysterious arrival of a new David.

The Hebrew text behind "triumphant and victorious" in Zech. 9:9 is expressed quite well in the NEB: "His cause won, his victory gained." The first of the two words (Hebrew *tsaddiq*) is often enough translated "the just one." It refers to Yahweh's justice towards himself and to his word by fulfilling divine promises in every respect. Thus the Lord is "triumphant" and "his cause won" (cf. Exod. 34:6-7). The other word in the RSV, "victorious," comes from the Hebrew word "to save," here in the passive mood; the Greek and most translations, however, render it in the active mood. The messianic king according to the Hebrew text is himself the servant and disciple of God, himself passively led along the way with infused strength and wisdom, himself receiving what he imparts to others, himself in full possession before sharing these with others. The messianic king is himself saved in the process of saving others. Zechariah deliberately intended this passive reading, for in relying upon another prophetic passage, he deliberatly changed the reading of this single word from the active to the passive:

> The Lord, your God, is in your midst,
>   a warrior *who gives victory;*
> He will rejoice over you with gladness,
>   he will renew you in his love.
>   (Zeph. 3:17)

"Who gives victory" is a single Hebrew word, here the active form, where Zech. 9:9 has the passive.

It is difficult to know if the next line of Zech. 9:9,

> *humble and riding on an ass*

should be pressed for a meaning of suffering and humiliation. The Hebrew word *'ny,* "humble," can mean "striken" or "afflicted," but it is also used with the generic sense of "humility." This word when united with the following phrase, "riding on an ass," connotes the peaceful entry of a king into a city. Asses or donkeys were the mount of princes who proceed in a friendly way through their domain: Gen. 49:11; Judg. 5:10; 2 Sam. 19:26; 1 Kgs. 1:33. Zechariah is reacting against the ostentatious splendor of preexilic kings, condemned by the prophets (Jer. 17:25).

The two kingdoms of Israel (Ephraim and Judah) will be reunited; the domain will reach out to that wide extent promised in the royal Davidic psalms (Ps. 72:8) and announced already in this section (Zech. 9:1-8; cf. 10:10-12). *Peace,* in the Hebrew sense of *shalom,* will bring wholeness, abundance, good health, the joyful blending of every good thing.

This passage may have prompted some of Jesus' actions in his triumphant entry into Jerusalem on Palm Sunday (Matt. 21:1-17). Typical of the NT, and especially of Matthew's Gospel, many OT texts overlap in this passage. On this occasion Jesus defends the children with their praise and shouting and reaches out to disabled people with healing power. Jesus recognizes in these lowly people not only a hope for a better way of life but also a conviction that this hope is realizable through God. These are not the folk to form a military machine against the enemy. They are helpless and passive, and in that capacity they sense in every pore of their body the overwhelming presence of God's saving activity. Jesus is centered in their midst, himself obedient to the will of the Father, as he will soon manifest upon the cross. In all these cases obedience meant courage, a summoning of one's total energy, a clear mindedness in seeking God, an appreciation of the Holy Scriptures and their direction, a compassionate outreach to others with whom to form the wholeness of *peace.*

THE DIVINE WARRIOR, PEACE TO JERUSALEM

Zechariah 9:11-17

This poem, an oracle of salvation at least in its first section, divides rather naturally between Zech. 9:11-13, the Lord's promises in his own name to help his people in captivity; vv. 14-15, the holy war fought by the Lord on the people's behalf; vv. 16-17, the victory celebration afterwards.

"The blood of my covenant" in v. 11 catches the eye of any Christian reader, for it appears only here in the OT and recurs in the eucharistic account of Mark's Gospel (Mark 14:24). With the help of such passages as Exod. 24:6-8 and Lev. 17:11, we understand that blood in these contexts does not designate death nor anything unclean but rather the living, pulsing element that unites, nourishes, and sustains all the organs of the human body. Sprinkled upon the altar as well as upon the people in Exod. 24, it symbolizes a union among the people themselves and altogether with the Lord. Blood, symbolizing life, naturally makes its claim upon life; it calls out for the reunion of all members of the family and of the people of God. God speaks its message in declaring: "I will set your captives free from the waterless pit."

The final phrase about "the waterless pit" follows almost verbatim the story of the patriarch Joseph, then a young boy, whom his jealous brothers "cast . . . into a pit [with] *no water in it*" (Gen. 37:24). We think as well of Jeremiah's imprisonment in a pit (Jer. 38:6-13). Cisterns for catching rain water abound in Israel, now as in ancient times, and were readily available as temporary jails. Israel did not have jails in our sense of the word. Aligning himself with these traditions, Zechariah is conscious of living with a pledge of their fulfillment in his own day. Thus the ancient word survived in a living, vibrant, meaningful way. Zechariah calls the people "prisoners of hope," whom he summons into "your stronghold." No matter how long they are caught in defeat and exile, due to their own sins, they can still be "prisoners of hope," from the assurance of the sacred and ancient word of God.

Zech. 9:13b is sometimes offered as evidence that the prophecy of chs. 9–14 was composed after the Greeks had invaded the land, either under Alexander the Great in 333 B.C. or else under his generals, who after his death ruled the land of Judah first from Alexandria in Egypt and after 190 from Antioch in Syria. First of all 9:13b breaks the meter and parallelism of the text and so may be a later addition; or else the Hebrew word for Greece here, *yawan,* according to Assyrian inscriptions of the 8th and 7th cents., refers to colonists from Greece along the coast of Asia Minor.

The holy war in vv. 14-15 bursts with the exuberant language of OT theophanies. Passages like Judg. 5:4; Hab. 3:3; and Ps. 18:14 echo here. The language of Zech. 9:15, "drink their blood like wine," is not as frightening in the Hebrew. The phrase "their blood" reads instead "make a din," "stagger," or as the JPSV expresses it, "They shall drink, shall rage as if with wine." This is metaphorical language for fury raging in time of battle.

The eschatological banquet, celebrating the Lord's victory amidst his people, is linked with the prophetical theme of "the day of the Lord." Now that the battle is over, the day of the Lord is no longer darkness but light, reversing Amos' words in Amos 5:18; nor is it "a day of distress and anguish, a day of ruin and devastation," as Zephaniah threatened (Zeph. 1:14-16). It has become a day when Israel, "like the jewels of a crown . . . shall shine on his land." The earth's fruitfulness is attributed to the Lord's mighty deeds in Israel's behalf. Salvation reaches joyfully to all aspects of life.

PROPHETIC WARNING
AGAINST SUPERSTITION
Zechariah 10:1-2

As a recognizable trademark of Zechariah, these lines resonate with many allusions to the earlier days of Israel, especially in prophecy. Zechariah drew upon warnings about the evils to expect for turning away from Yahweh, upon exhortations based on promises and the experience of true "consolation" from the Lord, not the "empty consolation" from diviners and dreamers.

This new section is carefully stitched into place by words and ideas from the preceding and following poems: i.e., in 10:1, the reference to rain and dryness is linked with 9:11; and the mention in 10:2 to evil shepherds prepares for v. 3.

Although idolatry seems to have been much less of a problem in postexilic Israel, still it surfaces in Isa. 56:9–57:13 in association with dreamers and evil leaders, and in Mal. 3:5. Evidently Israelites in the postexilic age were falling into the same trap as their ancestors. When Yahweh seemed to fail them and drought threatened their crops, they turned to pagan fertility gods for help. According to many biblical passages it is no one other than Yahweh who blesses his people in their faithfulness. The Lord provides them not only with a generous winter rain (Hebrew *geshem*) but also with the extra rain before and after the latter, called the autumn and spring rains (*yoreh* and *malqosh*; cf. Deut. 11:14; Hos. 6:3; Jer. 5:24; Joel 2:23). In this short poem even the winter rains had been sparse, and so the situation was desperate.

Hosea condemned the people for their prayers for rain if these were not accompanied with "steadfast love" and genuine "knowledge of God" (Hos. 6:6). After referring to "the rain in its season, the autumn rain and the spring rain," Jeremiah declared: "Your iniquities have turned these away, and your sins have kept good from you" (Jer. 5:25).

Rather than reform their ways, Israel was always tempted to blame Yahweh for this lack of rain and to turn to pagan gods of fertility or else to penetrate the hidden reasons of Yahweh (when the obvious one was already declared to them, their own sinfulness) by means of diviners and dreamers. Or they made use of teraphim, household gods that are mentioned as far back as Gen. 31:19 and reappear in 1 Sam. 15:23 and Ezek. 21:21. Diviners attempted to determine or predict the future by occult means: events rather obvious to everyone, whose secret meaning was released only to select persons who could "read" the twitching of animals' livers, the flight of birds, or the behavior of oil on top of water. These superstitious actions were condemned in Deut. 18:10-11.

Yet not all human means for determining God's will were outlawed. The use of the Urim and Thummim (some type of throwing dice) was sanctioned for the priests (Exod. 28:30; 1 Sam. 28:6). Dreams were sometimes the means of arriving at genuine knowledge from God: i.e., in Egypt Joseph was known as an interpreter of dreams (Gen. 40–41); or again in Amos 7:1-9; 8:1-2; 9:1-4 Yahweh communicates with the prophet through dreams or visions (cf. Zech. 1:7).

When we realize that some forms of divinization were acceptable ways of contacting Yahweh in biblical religion, then we see that the danger and the problem were all the more insidious. In condemning the prayer for early and late rains, Hosea was actually quoting from Israel's liturgy. The solution, therefore, does not lie in correct forms of ritual by legitimate priests or Levites, nor in saying the same prayers and offering the same sacrifices more frequently (cf. Amos 4:4-5; Isa. 43:22-28). The solution is interior, within reach of all sincere persons, if they respond to Yahweh's presence and listen to the words of the prophets about justice and sincerity. By contrast, in Amos 8:11-12 people will wander aimlessly, as in Zech 10:2, "to seek the word of the LORD [and] not find it."

Divinization, therefore, easily corrupted people and especially prophets, as Deut. 18:9-22 warned at quite some length. Superstition and greed (for the latter, see Mic. 3:5-8) turned out to be the principal sources of prophetic collapse, and as a result "the people [will] wander like sheep [and be] afflicted for want of a [true] shepherd" (Zech. 10:2).

YAHWEH'S HOLY WAR AND THE RETURN FROM EXILE

Zechariah 10:3-12

This section blends two types of writing: (1) *oracles from the Lord,* in the *first* person singular, which include the Lord's announcement of a holy war and his promise to bring back the exiled children of Israel and to resettle them in a promised land extending into Gilead and Lebanon (Zech. 10:3a, 6, 8-10); and (2) *prophetic speech,* which refers to Yahweh in the *third* person, promising true leadership and the Lord's subjugation of such mighty powers as Egypt and Assyria (vv. 3b-5, 7, 11-12). Both literary forms are carefully blended together. The entire poem was probably composed (or spoken) at one time, and for effectiveness the prophet moved from his own speech to the direct words of Yahweh. Examples of this are seen elsewhere in preexilic prophecy (i.e., Jer. 3:19-24).

The opening verse makes a skillful use of contrast, as it moves our attention from "my anger against . . . the shepherds" or false leaders of the people, to "the LORD of hosts [who] cares for his flock." The same strong employment of contrast occurs elsewhere in the poem (cf. v. 7 about "a mighty warrior" and "their children [who] shall . . . rejoice"), and again at the end of the poem, this time juxtaposing "the pride of Assyria . . . and the scepter of Egypt" with the way that "I will make [Israel] strong in the LORD."

Zechariah uses three metaphors for describing the true leaders whom the Lord will summon: *cornerstone,* leaders who will be stable and present to the people (Judg. 20:2; Isa. 19:13; Ps. 118:22); *tent peg,* a double image about a peg in the wall upon whom the people can lean for support (Isa. 22:23-24), or pegs in the ground for securing a tent so that it can be stretched taut and wide for a large family (Isa. 54:2); and *battle bow,* leaders who "symbolize fearless initiative in the Lord's cause" (2 Kgs. 13:17; Rev. 6:2) (cf. Joyce G. Baldwin, *Haggai, Zechariah, Malachi,* 174). While it is the Lord who raises up these ideal leaders, nonetheless, they still emerge "out of them," that is, out of the rank and file of the people who through faithful living and careful concern for their children generate such godly leaders.

The images of the holy war enter again into the poetry of Zechariah; the phrase "to sanctify a war" occurs in Mic. 3:5; Jer. 6:4; Joel 3:9. Because it is Yahweh alone who is battling, there is no question of Israel's marching soldiers into battle. The dimensions and consequences of this holy war, therefore, are more fearful, as they involve Yahweh in battle with demonic forces of evil across a universal panorama. While it is a question of "spiritual warfare," nonetheless it has real demands and real effects within Israel: fidelity, perseverance, and hope during the darkest of days as well as redemptive acts from Yahweh that completely transform Israel's existence. Imagery is drawn from such dramatic pieces of poetry as the Song of Moses in Exod. 15 and of Deborah in Judg. 5. Sometimes, as we saw already in the case of the RSV (Zech. 9:15) and now within 10:5, the translator has accentuated the violence beyond the scope of the Hebrew language. The verse should read *without* the bracketed material (which is rendered in the RSV): "trampling [the foe in] the mud of the streets"!

The final verse (10:12) regains its prophetic thrust if it reads:

I will make them strong in the LORD
and they shall *walk* in his name.

"To walk" (instead of 'glory,' RSV) brings the promise within the domain of everyday life and of one's routine responsibilities. Divine strength is required for this, so as to persevere over the long haul, especially through times of "holy warfare" till the Lord lays low "the pride of Assyria" and removes "the scepter of Egypt."

A TAUNT SONG OVER THE FALL OF ISRAEL'S ENEMIES

Zechariah 11:1-3

This transitional piece echoes the holy wars of Yahweh against the enemies of Israel, particularly those to the north and east. As in Zech. 9:1-8, the domain of the promised land must reach again its farthest limits. While the language is that of a lament, the occasion is the joyful collapse of Israel's enemies. Therefore, we call this piece a "taunt song." Not only are Lebanon to the north and Bashan to the east subjugated to God's will for Israel, but the wicked religious leaders within Israel, "the shepherds," are also wailing, "for their glory is despoiled!" The references to "the roar of the lions" and "the jungle of the Jordan" reflect lines in Amos 3:8 and Jer. 12:5. These lines may have been influenced by the memory of still another passage in Jeremiah:

> Wail, you shepherds, and cry, . . .
> For the LORD is despoiling their pasture,
>   and the peaceful folds are devastated, . . .
> Like a lion, he has left his covert. (Jer. 25:34-38)

As is frequently the case with poems about the holy war and with oracles against the nations, the Hebrew language sparkles brilliantly, with skillful repetition of words and sounds, with taunts and ridicule in the name of sorrow and lamentation, with sudden changes of images as trees wail aloud, and then human beings, shepherds, foreigners, and indigenous leaders within Israel mourn. To "open your doors," as the initial phrase declares, is to be flooded at once with mourning from the world of the mighty. Yet with the common folk of Israel there is supreme happiness!

If divine inspiration can impart such exquisite artistry to a scene of devastation, then out of the darkness there is emerging a hope for peace and new life. We must persevere through the transition. Part of that transition is the ordeal of evil leadership even within Israel. It is to that topic that the next major section of Second Zechariah turns.

SHEPHERD AND FLOCK:
WHAT EACH DESERVES
Zechariah 11:4-17

If the title to this section is enigmatic, so is this entire chapter of Zechariah. As usually happens, however, in the midst of generic and symbolical writing in the Bible, individual items remain obscure but the overall message shines clearly. In this case the prophet is declaring a truism of politics: people get the kind of leaders that they deserve. A biblical proverb catches the message: "It shall be like people, like priest" (Hos. 4:9). A prophecy of Isaiah expands the proverb so that each group suffers the fate of the other:

> And it shall be, as with the people, so with the priest;
> as with the slave, so with his master;
> as with the maid, so with her mistress;
> as with the buyer, so with the seller;
> as with the lender, so with the borrower;
> as with the creditor, so with the debtor.
> The earth shall be utterly laid waste.
>
> (Isa. 24:2-3a)

We add to the list of Isaiah: as with the shepherd, so with the flock; each gets what it deserves, its own type of leader or group, made to its own image.

GOD PREVAILS THROUGH HISTORY, YET BEYOND IT

Throughout this section the first person singular, "I," pounds at our consciousness. We are dealing with some type of autobiographical account or, better, a live discussion between the Lord and the prophet. God speaks in the first person to commission the prophet (Zech. 11:4-6); the prophet speaks in his own name of his obedience and then of his failure (vv. 7-14). God speaks again to send forth the prophet on a mission symbolic of what his failure means in a disastrous way to the people (vv. 15-17). This sequence of human failures, when fitted into the larger context of chs. 9–14, leads up to

133

a divine action of superhuman proportions. The final age of the world is being ushered in.

In 9:1–11:3 we already saw how world powers collapse before the humble, peaceful king; Yahweh leads his people through the dark wailing of dreamers and diviners into a home happy with the sound of children. In the chapters to be considered next, human failures and sorrows, even among the Lord's anointed ones (chs. 11–12), give way to the eschatological victory at the end of time (ch. 14). Whatever may have been the temple superstitions and venalities condemned in 10:1-2 and 11:5-6, the prophecy of Zechariah will conclude in the temple with the glorious, universal celebration of the Feast of Tabernacles.

A comparison can be made between Zech. 11:4-17 and the account of the call of the prophet Isaiah. This latter also leads to an announcement of failure, that "the heart of this people [will be] fat, their ears heavy, and their eyes shut, lest they see . . . hear . . . and understand [your message]" (Isa. 6:10). When Isaiah asks, "How long, O LORD?" the answer comes back: "until . . . the land is utterly desolate [and the LORD raises up] the holy seed [from] its stump" (Isa. 6:11-13). While Zech. 11 ends with another rejection of the prophet, the prophecy as a whole has an optimistic end that the Lord achieves marvelously.

History, it seems, must run its course, exhaust its strength, and violently betray its best talents in order for men and women to realize what the prophet Isaiah had declared: only if one's faith is firm will God confirm that salvation comes through God alone (cf. Isa. 7:9b). Only by interacting closely with history does one become convinced that the goal is beyond history. Zechariah here emphasizes this position of Isaiah in his own way. By close literary parallels the prophet weaves together the ideas of Zech. 11:4-17 according to the pattern of the preceding section, but in reverse. What worked through God's intervention in the person of the humble king (9:1–11:3) does not succeed when undertaken by the best efforts of the prophet. We here expand upon the dissimilarities already provided by Rex A. Mason (*The Books of Haggai, Zechariah and Malachi,* 105):

9:1–11:3	11:4-17
poetry	almost all prose
optimistic	pessimistic
second and third person accounts	first person account

salvation for all	judgment against all
public oracles and announce-ments	private conversation between Yahweh and the prophet
divine leadership succeeds	human leadership fails

Another link between the two sections is recognized in the many allusions to shepherds and their flock in 9:16; 10:2, 3, 8-9; 11:3. Yet Yahweh is leading history forward so that "on that day" (11:11) of the eschatological moment, history collapses before the fearful and victorious presence of Yahweh. This prophetic message is fearsome: our best efforts are not sufficient. It is also reassuring: God brings our best efforts to a fulfillment greater than our dreams.

RELIGIOUS LEADERSHIP

While this section deals mostly with people who betray their role of leadership and turn it into a personal career for their own advantage, nonetheless, we can also look at the positive side of what is being condemned. We are also given a glimpse of postexilic Israelites in their small country of Yehud (the Aramaic form of Judah).

Leadership is always in a fragile situation, for eventually over a long period of time it depends for its success upon its acceptance by the people. People have a way of stubbornly resisting dictators and of asserting themselves. Although it is not evident at first, 11:4 introduces an idea that the people are a "flock doomed [by their own devices] to slaughter," because they have chosen to betray the one person capable of helping them. This conclusion is corroborated by a comparison with Jeremiah. The word "slaughter," frequent enough in the Hebrew Bible, is seldom found in the form right here. The only other identical occurrence is seen in the prophecy of Jeremiah:

Pull them out like sheep for the slaughter,
and set them apart for the day of slaughter.
(Jer. 12:3)

These lines, within a poem called the first confession, see Jeremiah arguing with God, sensing not only betrayal from close relatives but also silent desertion by God. The agony is intense. The surrounding verses of the first confession portray: (1) "the men of Anathoth [Jeremiah's hometown], who seek your life, and say, 'Do not prophesy in the name of the LORD'" (Jer. 11:21); and (2) "your brothers and the house of your father, [who] have dealt treacherously with you; they are in full cry after you" (Jer. 12:6). In Zechariah's case, he too is betrayed by those close to him (Zech. 13:2-6). When punishment comes upon the people, because of their infidelity and selfishness, the prophet is caught within it. He may have saved himself by fleeing away, but desertion follows the selfish and cowardly style of the hireling (cf. John 10:12).

Leadership ultimately depends upon the agreement of others to follow. For the leader, accordingly, there are solitary moments of rejection and seeming failure. Perhaps what is more searing for the prophet than personal rejection and failure is the sight of one's fellow Israelites "doomed to slaughter" (Zech. 11:4). Only the next generation of followers will recognize the foolishness of their ancestors and the heroic wisdom of the earlier prophet. They will assent to true prophecy in the one rejected by their forebears; they will include the prophetical message within their sacred and inspired tradition. True leadership bears the mark of perseverance through long solitary moments.

In the following verse (v. 5) Zechariah recalls a page from earlier prophets who condemned wealthy people not just for getting wealthier but for doing it at a painful cost to the poor. As a result, these latter were being forced into slavery. Zechariah hears the Lord speak against calloused and greedy people who manipulate privilege and power. They even make a satirical stab at piety:

> Those who buy them slay them and go unpunished; and those who sell them say, "Blessed be the LORD, I have become rich."

Amos condemned those people of Israel who "sell the righteous for silver, and the needy for a pair of shoes" (Amos 2:6). In order to insure compliance that debts be paid in full, a poor man is sold into slavery for a debt equal to a pair of shoes. The law of humanity is violated to keep the law of bookkeepers and financial agents. The prophet Micah has other biting passages of outrage (cf. Mic. 2:2-3, 8-9; 3:1-3, 9-12), as do other prophets (cf. Isa. 5:8-30; Ezek. 34:2-3).

We learn from Nehemiah that people were still selling fellow Jews into slavery even in the postexilic age of Zechariah. In order to obtain necessary food and pay the Persian taxes, the poor cry out in muffled desperation:

> We are forcing our sons and our daughters to be slaves, and some of our daughters have already been enslaved; but it is not

in our power to help it, for other men have our fields and our vineyards. (Neh. 5:5)

It is interesting to note that the list of temple personnel included not only "the priests, the Levites, the gatekeepers, [and] the singers," but also "the temple servants" (Neh. 7:73). "Servants" is a more euphemistic way of translating the same Hebrew word, "slave," as is done in the NAB.

Joyce G. Baldwin (*Haggai, Zechariah, Malachi,* 180) draws an inference from the feminine gender pronoun, "those who buy *them* slay *them*" (Zech. 11:5). The example is drawn from slaughtering female animals that were normally intended for breeding purposes rather than for food. This self-indulgent, crass people will stop at nothing in pampering themselves.

And they say, "Blessed be the LORD, I have become rich!" The former phrase may be an example of a *tiqqun sopherim,* "a correction of the scribes," to avoid the scandalous statement, actually spoken, "Cursed be the Lord" (cf. Job 2:9, which is translated "Curse God, and die," but actually reads in the Hebrew "Bless God and die"). For these people in Zechariah's day religion has become a joke! Or is it an example of the easy way by which some people can avoid serious responsibility by turning the conversation into misplaced humor? True leadership is not only compassionate toward the poor and needy but it thus manifests its sincere devotion toward God and religious practice.

The next phrase in Zech. 11:5 reaches the depth of abject venality in the priests and false shepherds, who "have no pity on [the poor]." They will tolerate such injustice because they are receiving generous stipends from wealthy, greedy people. Micah already spoke about priests and temple prophets who proclaim "Shalom!" when their teeth have something to bite but who sanctify war when one puts little or nothing into their mouths (Mic. 3:5).

Still another aspect of true leadership can be detected in Zechariah's symbolic action with the two shepherd staffs, named "Grace" and "Union" (Zech. 11:7, 10, 14). Leaders according to God's directions strive to keep the people, first within the continuity and tradition of the Covenant, symbolized by the staff named "Grace," and second within the bonds of loyalty among themselves, symbolized by the staff named "Union." The Hebrew word for *grace* (*no'am;* cf. Ruth's mother-in-law, Naomi, Ruth 1:2) occurs in Ps. 27:4 within the context of God's presence in the temple:

One thing have I asked of the Lord,
. . .that I may dwell in the house of the Lord
all the days of my life,
to behold *the beauty* of the Lord,
and to inquire in his temple.

The same association of the word with covenant graces is seen in Ps. 90:17.

The name of the other staff, *Union,* as we see explicitly in Zech. 11:14, stands for the bond between the north and the south, the former kingdoms of Israel and Judah, which Zechariah hoped to see restored. The prophet Ezekiel used a similar example; he joined two sticks together, one with the inscription "For Judah," and the other with the inscription "For Joseph" (Ezek. 37:16-18). Ezekiel sees members of these tribes coming "from the nations among which they have gone" and they will become "one nation" with "one king." Ezekiel is not necessarily extending this offer to those who remained behind in the land of Israel and did not go into exile. As we saw in the introduction to the books of Haggai and First Zechariah, great antagonism separated those who returned from exile from those who had been left behind in the land. The question remains open: is Zechariah here inviting the returnees to open the temple and their covenant to the people of the land, or is he going no further than Ezekiel? He was seeking at least some kind of bonding with people from the former kingdom of Israel.

Authentic leadership according to the statement in Zech. 11 not only sought a reestablishment of the covenant with Yahweh and a bonding in God of the people among themselves, but the prophet also called upon the leaders themselves to be united and to work together peacefully. Yet this is not peace at any cost, especially at the cost of the poor and defenseless, victimized, as we have seen, by the false shepherds at Jerusalem. With profound regret Zechariah sees a collapse of what the prophet Ezekiel had enunciated about the good shepherd. The unfortunate results, like the dependence upon Ezekiel, seem rather clear (cf. Paul D. Hanson, *The Dawn of Apocalyptic,* 344):

Ezek. 34	Zech. 11
Yahweh saves (vv. 9-16)	Yahweh scatters (v. 6)
promise of a shepherd who feeds them (v. 23)	promise of a shepherd who opposes them (v. 16)
covenant of peace (v. 25)	covenant is broken (vv. 10, 14)

| blessings (vv. 26-31) | doom and desolation (v. 16) |
| eschatological age at hand | eschatological age is delayed |

True leadership has a lasting ability to survive those bleak times when earlier hopes, genuinely from God, are thwarted and their fulfillment postponed by God. Leadership does not force its timetable upon God but patiently waits upon the Lord (cf. Isa. 7:4; 30:15-18).

HISTORICAL IDENTIFICATION AND NEW TESTAMENT FULFILLMENT

As stated at the beginning of this section, Zech. 11:4-17 is among the most obscure passages in the OT. Our interpretation here respected the obscurity and offered an interpretation generic enough to give us insights into the experiences of the prophet and into leadership of any age. The NT turned to an enigmatic section like this one in presenting important moments in the life and ministry of Jesus. Evidently the NT writers, in quoting from a passage textually and interpretively uncertain, are not trying to prove a point against doubters or adversaries. Because of a connection between obscurity and contemplation, biblical writers are inviting us to prolonged, silent prayer for receiving God's message. We need to search for ways to clarify the meaning, because even a limited light leads to new depths of wonder before God.

One of the puzzling statements occurs in v. 8, "In one month I destroyed the three shepherds." Long ago in 1912 when writing in the *International Critical Commentary,* H. G. T. Mitchell wrote:

> There are at least forty [conjectures on this subject], together covering the whole field of Hebrew history from the Exodus to the conquest of Palestine by the Romans, and including most of the men and institutions therein of any importance. (*Haggai and Zechariah,* 306)

Here we interpret "three" as a number symbolical of completion (cf. Gen. 42:18; Exod. 19:11, 16; Josh. 3:2; Isa. 16:14; Hos. 6:2). Zechariah quickly removed "in one month" three, that is, *all* false leaders standing in the way of religious reform. While the RSV speaks of *destroying* the three shepherds, the Hebrew word is better translated "did away with" (NAB) or "removed" (Ralph L. Smith, *Micah—Malachi,* 268).

Particularly because of the NT parallel in the account of Jesus' passion and death, the identification of still another phrase has aroused much curiosity: "my wages thirty shekels of silver." In Matt. 26:15 "thirty pieces of silver" were given by the temple priests to Judas Iscariot. In Matt. 27:5-10 Judas threw down "the pieces of silver in the temple" before "he went and hanged himself," silver that the temple priests used to purchase "the potter's field," thus fulfilling "what had been spoken by the prophet Jeremiah." (For the naming of Jeremiah here instead of Zechariah, see below.) For another account of Judas' death and the naming of the field as "Akeldama," see Acts 1:15-20.

"Thirty shekels of silver" is sometimes interpreted as an impressive sum (the tax of forty shekels in Neh. 5:15 was considered quite burdensome) or as ignominious (the price of a slave in Exod. 21:32) or as small enough (all of two hundred shekels of silver was used in Judg. 17:4 for making a statue). Peter L. Ackroyd remarks: "The significance of the payment is lost, unless it reappears in 13:9" (§ 571g). Even though the Persians introduced currency (from a policy already initiated at Sardis in Asia Minor), nonetheless, during most of biblical history the shekel was more a standard of weight, and this practice continued in the temple. Note that the text correctly reads, "they *weighed out* as my wages thirty shekels of silver."

Enormous discussion has gone into the phrase of Zech. 11:13, "Cast it into *the treasury.*" The Hebrew word *yotser* generally means "a potter" who is working with clay; the Greek LXX understood the money to be thrown "into the furnace." Almost all commentators adopt the explanation of C. C. Torrey, "The Foundry of the Second Temple at Jerusalem," *JBL* 55 (1936): 247-260, which established the existence of foundries at temples that were used for smelting the coins and offerings presented to the temple. The worker in charge of the operation was designated *yotser.* Elsewhere in the Bible this Hebrew word refers to someone working with metal (cf. Exod. 32:2-4, 24; Isa. 44:9-10). Temples functioned as storehouses for precious things (Josh. 6:24; Ezra 2:6-11) and even as banks (2 Macc. 3:9-40).

In quoting this passage from Zechariah, Matthew (Matt. 27:9-10) also refers to a prophetic action of Jeremiah, who purchased the family plot of land at Anathoth for "seventeen shekels of silver" (Jer. 32:9) and possibly to Jeremiah's visit to the potter (Jer. 18:2). Jeremiah's purchase of the homestead, during a break in the Babylonian siege of Jerusalem, was meant as a symbolic way of prophesying the future security of God's people in their own land. Its place within Jer. 30–33, a brief book of consolation, assures this interpretation. Matthew attributes everything to the better known prophet, Jeremiah (cf. Mark 1:2-3, where a blend of Mal. 3:1 and Isa. 40:3 is given under the single name of Isaiah).

The overall momentum of OT prophecy, certainly in the final editing of each book, is toward a happy conclusion. In Zech. 9–14 God will victoriously transform a devastated area with new life. Likewise Matthew's Gospel, in drawing upon prophecy in an account of Jesus' suffering and death, is already anticipating the resurrection. Again for Jesus himself and through Jesus for us, sorrow and death lead to a new, happy life that is final and eternal.

Suffering and rejection, however, come first. In this context we remark about the word in 11:7 and 11 translated "traffickers" or "merchants." This reading is a slight emendation of the Hebrew and is dependent upon the reading of the Greek LXX, "Canaanites." The original meaning of this latter word was "merchants" (Job 41:6; Prov. 31:24; Zech. 14:21). The Hebrew text reads literally "the poor." This reading emphasizes the lowly condition of the people or the flock, and therefore seems congenial to the overall setting, not only in Zechariah but also in the application of this passage to Jesus' suffering and death in the Gospel of Matthew.

THE NEW COVENANT
THROUGH VICTORY OVER
THE NATIONS, CLEANSING,
AND MOURNING

Zechariah 12:1–13:9

After a solemn introduction to chs. 12–14 in the opening verse (12:1), this section runs on a double track, the second subsection being in many ways a repeat of the first:

(1)	12:2-9	Judah and Jerusalem are cleansed of foreign invaders
(2)	12:10–13:1	Mourning at Jerusalem over the beloved martyr(s)
(1a)	13:2-6	Cleansing the temple of false prophets and their idols
(2a)	13:7-9	Martyrdom of the shepherd and the renewal of the Covenant for the remnant

Several key words or concepts knit these sections together: (1) *the day of the Lord* ("on that day"): 12:3, 4, 6, 8, 9, 11; 13:1, 2, 4 (absent in 13:7-9, one of the reasons why many scholars transfer the latter verses to the end of 11:4-17 about the shepherds); (2) *strike:* 12:4 (twice); 13:6 (as a noun, 'wounds'), 7; (3) *laceration:* 12:3, 10; 13:6, 7.

In the tradition of the preexilic prophets this section envisages the future of Judah and Jerusalem in relation to the rest of the world, even if it means the defeat of other nations, but it shows the *Zeitgeist* of the postexilic age by centering the new age within the temple and even drawing important vocabulary from its ritual. The early prophetic tradition about "the day of the Lord," first encountered clearly in the preaching of Amos (Amos 5:18), continues to dominate this section up to Zech. 13:6 inclusively. Prophetic suffering, ever more evident with Jeremiah and turned into a theology of redemption in Isa. 40–55, leaves its mark of tears in Zech. 12:10-14 and 13:7. Again we realize that prophecy in its development from one age to another draws its nourishment from tap roots in tradition. Finally, the postexilic situation of unworthy temple personnel who even tolerated idolatry, evident in other literature of this age (cf. 11:4-17; Isa. 57), blatantly reappears here. It seems that it can never be totally eradicated.

SOLEMN INTRODUCTION
Zechariah 12:1

The phrase "An Oracle" (Hebrew *massa'*), sets chs. 12–14 apart as it does chs. 9–11 and Mal. 1–3 (cf. Zech. 9:1). A fragment of a hymn, honoring Yahweh the Creator, enhances this introduction. The hymnic quality is perceived in the Hebrew use of participles:

> stretching out the heavens,
> establishing the earth,
> forming the human spirit within.

These creative actions are attributed to "the Word of the LORD." Israel's obedience enables God's omnipotent word to achieve the purpose for which it has been spoken and sent forth (cf. Isa. 55:11).

We are reminded not only of hymnic lines in the introduction to other prophetic books (Amos 1:2; Mic. 1:2-4) but also of the hymnic fragments that an editor stitched three times into place within the prophecy of Amos (Amos 4:13; 5:8; 9:5-6). The first of these is quite close to the introductory hymn for Zech. 12–14. Editing such as this reemphasizes for us the role of the temple personnel and ritual in the preservation of prophetic literature, despite all their faults as evidenced in the preceding section about false shepherds.

In these hymns, as well as in some of the earliest psalms (cf. Pss. 8, 19A, 29, 104), there appears a strong faith in Yahweh as Lord of creation. These same psalms and prophetic fragments show considerable resemblance to the mythology of neighboring, non-Israelite religions. Although the polytheism and other mythological excesses have been washed out of most of the lines in Isa. 40–55 and in postexilic literature such as Zechariah, nonetheless the important contribution of the nations to the religion of Israel ought not to be overlooked. This temptation to bypass the nations is felt especially in passages of Zechariah where the nations are reduced to panic and defeat.

VICTORY OVER THE NATIONS
Zechariah 12:2-9

Typical of almost every line in the prophecies of Haggai and especially of Zechariah, this poem echoes earlier biblical ideas and words. This poem, which presents a dramatic battle with the nations and a completely new day for Israel, is best appreciated through tradition. Earlier prophecies summoned the angry, destructive armies of the nations against Israel; these prophetic pieces, however, were leading to a day of fulfillment. With the dawning of *that day,* a prophet like Zechariah steps forward and guides the people according to the preaching of Amos, Isaiah, Zephaniah, and other prophets. All of these books end happily. Without this guidance the cataclysmic battles of Zech. 12 and 14 would leave Israel with all the world in chaos. We cite these many contacts with tradition:

Jerusalem, center of world conflict: Pss. 46–48; Isa. 10:5-19; Ezek. 38:1-23

cup of reeling: Jer. 25:15; Isa. 51:17; Hab. 2:16

a heavy stone: Isa. 28:16

strike with panic and blindness: Deut. 28:28

a blazing pot: Jer. 1:13

feeblest among them like David: 2 Sam. 5:6-8

Several questions come to mind as we review the case of Jerusalem as the center of world conflict and as a city inviolable and eternal. First of all, why would the prophet or the people still have such faith in the holy city, in view of its total destruction by the Babylonians in 587 B.C.? This devastation was all the more baffling for Israel to deal with, because a false hope about the city's impregnable defenses had grown up before the Exile. When Jerusalem was preserved in 701 from the ferocious military might of the Assyrians, the event was remembered in songs of exalted joy (e.g., Isa. 14:24-27 and especially 17:12-14). This belief that God had wondrously preserved the city gave rise to the account that *"the angel of the Lord* went forth and struck down one hundred and eighty-five thousand in the Assyrian camp" (Isa. 37:36 NAB). That this statement is to be interpreted *symbolically* of *Yahweh's* direction of history and in this case of Jerusalem's salvation, we note a different explanation about Jerusalem's destruction in Isa. 1:4-8 and 22:5-11 (cf. Ronald E. Clements, *Isaiah and the Deliverance of Jerusalem*).

This same understanding about indestructible Jerusalem is reflected in the preexilic Songs of Korah (Pss. 46–48). This trilogy in honor of Jerusalem is introduced in the title to Ps. 46 with the phrase, "according to Alamoth." The final Hebrew word can be separated to read *'al moth*, "beyond death." It then forms an "inclusion" with an identical phrase at the end of the trilogy in the final verse of Ps. 48, *'al muth*, translated "for ever" (RSV). So strong was the faith of priests and temple prophets in Jerusalem's eternal protection by God that they wanted to execute the prophet Jeremiah for preaching differently (Jer. 26:11).

Yet, true to the threat of Jeremiah, the city was leveled to the ground as if it had been Sodom and Gomorrah (cf. Isa. 1:9). Not only with the memory but also with evident signs of Jerusalem's destruction before one's eyes, how can the prophet Zechariah speak again of its inviolability in face of attack from "all the peoples round about [and] all the nations of the earth" (Zech. 12:2-3)? It seems that destruction produced a still stronger faith in Jerusalem's inviolability. This almost contradictory phemomenon is partially explained by the way prophecy ended upbeat with the sighting of a new Jerusalem at the end of the books of Isaiah and Zechariah. The question is discussed at length by Robert P. Carroll, *When Prophecy Failed*.

We can discuss the same question from another viewpoint, that of the nations: why would they be bothering about the tiny city of postexilic Jerusalem? If Zech. 12 comes from a period before Nehemiah (therefore, before 445), then the city walls are not yet constructed and the number of inhabitants is minimal. In response, we recognize that Zechariah is writing *theologically* about the history of Jerusalem and is centering all peoples and nations around Yahweh, enthroned in the Jerusalem temple as king (cf. Pss. 96–99). Theology is not divorced from military and political reality, no matter how much the latter may ignore it or even despise it. Even in our century, atheistic countries such as Soviet Russia find themselves obliged to deal with the state of Israel and its capital at Jerusalem!

Jerusalem represents God's determination to unite all peoples and nations under one divine plan of peace. Jerusalem with its history of heroic survivals through immense dangers and horrendous destructions offers more than enough evidence that this faith is solidly based.

Some ambiguity is introduced into this poem by the references to "the clans of Judah" (Zech. 12:5-6) and "the tents of Judah" (v. 7) as a group distinct from Jerusalem and its local inhabitants. The former, according to Zechariah, are the first to receive victory from the Lord and to devour the nations "like a blazing pot [and] a flaming torch" (v. 6). They provide a "shield about the inhabitants of Jerusalem," protecting it from the invaders (v. 8). Do these passages represent an attitude favoring the countryside over metropolitan Jerusalem? Such a position was argued by Micah against the unjust policies of the capital city of Jerusalem. We meet it again in the early postexilic period among the people of the land who had never gone into exile and were being repudiated by the returnees. While the prophecy of Zechariah generally sides with the Jerusalem temple and its priesthood, nonetheless, it is likely that the prophet takes a discreet, more traditionally prophetic stance of independence, particularly in chs. 9–14.

Zechariah does not go to the extreme position of such passages as Isa. 55:3-5 (from the time of the Exile), in which the eternal promises for David are returned to the people at large. In fact, Zech. 12:8b refers to "the house of David [which] shall be like God, like the angel of the LORD." Some commentators hold that the second phrase about the angel of the Lord was added to weaken the bold expression of being "like God" (Robert C. Dentan, *IB* 6:1107; Peter R. Ackroyd, § 571j; Édouard P. Dhorme, *La Bible,* 865). Because these references represent the last gasp of Davidic royalty in the Bible, they are all the more important for Zechariah's determination not to lose this important tradition.

THE GREAT LAMENTATION
Zechariah 12:10–13:1

While this passage is marred with textual problems and historical obscurity, it remains one of the most frequently quoted OT texts in the NT. The textual difficulties show up in the central verse:

> . . . so that, when they *look on him whom they have pierced,* they shall mourn for him, as one mourns for an only child, and weep bitterly over him, as one weeps over a first-born. (12:10 RSV)

The italicized words read in the Hebrew: "look *on me* whom they have pierced." This first person reading occurs only here; the rest of the verse reads in the third person, "mourn for *him* . . . weep bitterly over *him.*" The Hebrew reading is followed by all ancient versions: i.e., the LXX, the Old Latin, the Vulgate, the Syriac, the Targum. Yet the NT citations read, in the third person, "look on him" (John 19:37; Rev. 1:7). An explanatory rendition of the Hebrew text, offered by J. D. W. Watts ("Zechariah," *The Broadman Bible Commentary* 7:357) and in agreement with Édouard P. Dhorme (*La Bible,* 865-66), Matthias Delcor ("Un problème de critique textuelle et d'exégèse: Zach., XII, 10," *RB* 58 [1951]: 192), and Douglas R. Jones (*Haggai, Zechariah and Malachi,* 161) reads:

> when they look "to me" (in prayer) "regarding" (those) whom they (the nations) have pierced (i.e., soldiers of Judah), they shall mourn for him (a collective).

This explanation is open to the messianic interpretation of the NT and long Christian tradition. Jesus is at the end of a long series of martyrs and witnesses (cf. Heb. 12:1-4). We will find that the NT refines what has been the continuous Jewish understanding from the time of Zechariah.

Judaism glories in its martyrs and suffering servants. The reference in Zech. 12:11 to the plain of Megiddo reminds us of the tragic death of the reforming King Josiah for whom "all Judah and Jerusalem mourned [and] Jeremiah also uttered a lament" (2 Chr.

35:24-25). Jeremiah himself was a figure of sadness and rejection
(cf. Jer. 12:1-6; 15:10-21; 20:7-18), whose sustaining influence is
felt in the songs of the suffering servant (Isa. 49:1-7; 50:4-9; and
esp. 52:13–53:12) and still later in the book of Job (Job 3:11;
10:18-19). This attitude resonates plaintively and then triumphantly
in Ps. 22. All of these texts prepared for an acceptance, not necessarily an understanding, of sorrow and even death on the part of just
people as a way toward the fulfillment of God's promises. It is not
unthinkable that the Messiah, the ideal representative of this long
tradition, should achieve his mission through suffering and death.

The Babylonian Talmud interprets Zech. 12:10 messianically
when it comments on "the cause of the slaying of Messiah the son of
Joseph [footnote from the same text: 'the precursor of the Messiah
ben David, the herald of the true Messianic age'] that well agrees
with the scriptural verse, *and they shall look upon me because they have
thrust him through, and they shall mourn for him as one mourneth for his
only son*" (Seder Mo'ed, Sukkah 51b–52a; Soncino edition, 246-47).

The NT, we repeat, stands in a long tradition that God's final
victory for the chosen people does not happen easily but is the result
of completely unselfish dedication and of the willingness to die that
new life may emerge gloriously. Yet even in the victory we do not
completely forget the cost. In heaven the just will still recognize on
Jesus the scars of the crucifixion (cf. Rev. 1:7).

While victory is assured in Zech. 9–14, nonetheless, the mourning is intense as well as intimate, "as . . . for an only child, . . . a first-
born." The reference to "the house of David [and] the house of
Nathan [and] the house of Levi [and] the family of the Shimeites"
is not totally clear, even though the general meaning of a great
lamentation throughout the land is unmistakable. According to two
different interpretations the text is referring *either* to the family of
two royal personages (David and his son Nathan, 1 Chr. 14:4) and
to two priestly personages (Levi and his grandson Shimei, Num.
3:16-18; 1 Chr. 6:16-17), *or* to a representative of the four principal classes of biblical tradition: the royal (David, 1 Sam. 16:1-13),
the prophetic (Nathan, 2 Sam. 7:2), the priestly (Levi, Deut. 33:8-
11), and the sapiential (Shimei, 1 Kgs. 4:18, a difficult reference).

So universal is this sorrow that even "the land shall mourn"
(Zech. 12:12). In this context the prophet refers to "the [great]
mourning for Hadadrimmon in the plain of Megiddo." The reference is probably to the Phoenician storm god Hadad, patron of fertility who died and revived according to the dry and rainy seasons
and whose worship must have been a prominent temptation where

the pass of Megiddo opens into the breadbasket plain of Jezreel (which means "God sows"; cf. Hos. 1:4; 2:21-23). Even here there is desolation and draught. In reverse order, however, the end of the great lamentation will lead to fertility and abundance through the blessing of Yahweh, when the messianic Feast of Tabernacles is celebrated (Zech. 14:16-19).

These references to pagan and Jewish ritual bring us to consider a final aspect of the Great Lamentation. There is a pervasive liturgical or cultic tone to the entire section, brought to our attention by Matthias Delcor, *RB* 58 (1951): 194-95. Delcor considers the parallels with Ezek. 36. In the latter passage, Ezekiel is announcing the new heart and the new covenant for Israel. The following are some of the details to be found in each:

> defilement and uncleanness; pouring out wrath and later clean, purifying water; a new spirit of grace and life; profaning God's holy name; famine or fertility; renewal of the covenant formula, "I am your God, you are my people."

These links with Ezekiel as well as these allusions to ritual indicate Zechariah's firm and congenial loyalty to the Jerusalem temple. Finally the "fountain opened for the house of David and the inhabitants of Jerusalem" (Zech. 13:1) brings us into contact with a host of biblical passages for blessings. These flow from God's presence in the temple like a stream of living, fresh water (Isa. 12:3; Ezek. 47:1-12; Joel 3:18; Ps. 46:4). Rather than necessarily refer to these passages as messianic, it may be closer to the truth to see in them a pattern by which worship in God's presence surrounds the worshipper with the total reality of life, possible only in faithful union with God. An example of this is seen in Sir. 24, where even the four rivers of paradise flow from a single source in the temple!

CLEANSING THE TEMPLE
OF FALSE PROPHETS
Zechariah 13:2-6

With a nostalgic pang of sorrow in our heart we read this "death certificate" of classical prophecy. Once the institution was represented by such giants as Amos and Hosea, Isaiah and Jeremiah before the Exile, Ezekiel and Second Isaiah during the Exile. We already noticed with Haggai and the earlier parts of Zechariah that a new breed of prophets has appeared. They are closely aligned with temple and priesthood, and in Hag. 2:10-15, they deferred to the priests for answering inquiries. It is not that postexilic priesthood was that much purer than prophecy in God's eyes; we have already seen the priestly excesses in Zech. 11:4-17 and the need for purification in the case of the high priest Joshua (ch. 3). Prophecy, however, does not have the staying power of priesthood and therefore is much more vulnerable. Prophecy is not a permanent institution like other offices in biblical religion, i.e., Levites and priests, elders and judges.

We can chart the decline in prophecy in several independent sources. Nehemiah condemns the prophet Shemaiah for trying to discourage him and induce him to flee the country. He asks the Lord to "remember [to their punishment] also the prophetess Noadiah and the rest of the prophets who wanted to make me afraid" (Neh. 6:10-14).

The prophets will attempt to deny that they are prophets, yet all the while act by their "unclean spirit" and even at times put on the "hairy mantle" of a prophet. They continue to slash themselves in their fanatic orgies (cf. 1 Kgs. 18:28) and then pretend that the scars or tattoos were inflicted on them by traitors in their own homes! Even their own parents will not acknowledge these greedy, sensual people who manipulate religion for their own secret gain. They quote the words of the prophet Amos deceitfully to declare that they are not prophets but men who work the soil (cf. Amos 7:14-15).

MARTYRDOM, RENEWAL, AND REMNANT

Zechariah 13:7-9

Following the lead of such scholars as Peter R. Ackroyd ("Zechariah," § 572a), Robert C. Dentan (*IB* 6:1109), Douglas R. Jones (*Haggai, Zechariah and Malachi,* 168-69), Ralph L. Smith (*Micah—Malachi,* 283) and Édouard P. Dhorme (*La Bible,* cxii-cxiii), we do not transfer this short section to the end of 11:4-17 (also about good and evil shepherds) but rather take up the passage right here. In this case the reference is to a good shepherd who suffers from abuse, perhaps from mortal blows, with the consequent scattering of the flock of Israel. Already in chs. 12–13 Zechariah has spoken of the nations whose destruction leads to a new Jerusalem, to the martyred servant mourned with great lamentation, and to the false prophets. Evidently there is no easy way to arrive at the purity and goodness that characterize the kingdom of God among his people. These lines summarize what has already been said about hopes, betrayal, sorrows, and revival of true leadership.

No adequate explanation is offered why the good people must suffer along with the wicked for the sins of the wicked. For that matter, not even the long book of Job satisfactorily answered this question! History has shown many times over that suffering which scatters and bewilders ends up with a power to purify and create a remnant of faithful followers. Once again Zechariah speaks with many echoes of earlier prophetical pieces. Our attention is drawn particularly to Isa. 1:21-26, in which Jerusalem is purified like silver, as the Lord "will smelt away your dross . . . and remove all your alloy, and . . . you shall be called [again] the city of righteousness, the faithful city."

The covenant is renewed with a variation of the customary formula: I am their God, they are my people (cf. Ezek. 36:28; Jer. 31:1, 33).

This passage about striking the shepherd and scattering the flock occurs several times in the NT, quoted in Mark 14:27 as Jesus was making his way to the garden of Gethsemane. Other passages about sheep without a shepherd (Mark 6:34; Matt. 9:36) come to mind.

Against the background of Zechariah, a clear enough note is sounded. The scattering is only a passage toward a goal when the Lord's most loyal disciples will be gathered together again. For this and other reasons, Zech. 13:7-9 carries a messianic message of victory and salvation. Again, however, this completion comes only through a mysterious way where the elect seem to wander without the shepherd. Actually they are being led ever more firmly through the intuitions inspired by the Lord's interior presence with them.

In conclusion to the larger section of 12:1–13:9, we recognize that while it is more cultic than, for instance, the eschatological poems of Isa. 24–27, it is less cultic and less temple oriented than Ezekiel, 1-2 Chronicles, and Joel. The movement is much more in the direction of the apocalyptic with its extreme symbolism; we are being prepared for the final chapter of Zechariah. Zechariah 12:1–13:9 is much more symbolic than 1-2 Chronicles. Finally, we take note of the ambivalence of Zechariah toward the nations. Some passages seem quite favorable, but others totally reject them. In this sense Zechariah is in line with most of the OT. It never provides anything more than signals; a complete theology of universal salvation is not to be found here, for nowhere is the salvation of the nations linked with other key theological motifs of Judaism, such as the temple, election, priesthood, and promised land. Some of these ideas, nonetheless, will be advanced in the final chapter of Zechariah.

THE FINALE:
APOCALYPTIC AND CULTIC

Zechariah 14:1-21

The prophecy of Zechariah ends in the pattern of the earlier chapters, centering as it does on Jerusalem as the focus of world history, the goal of pilgrimage, and the place of liturgical celebration. Chapter 14, however, intensifies the style of the preceding sections and manifests a vigorous apocalyptic form. As always, biblical speakers and writers draw upon the past, but they develop the earlier traditions in new directions as they chart a way through their own problems and hopes.

LITURGY, A CELEBRATION TODAY
OF PAST PROMISES AND FUTURE HOPES

We have grown accustomed to problems with the meaning of Hebrew words in the book of Zechariah; again the words and phrases are obscure enough that we are frequently in doubt about a precise translation. Yet, as was previously the case, the overall structure and principal message seem clear enough. A key phrase, "day of the Lord" (or "on that day"), knits the pieces together, as happened in 12:1–13:9. This prophetic motif rings out in 14:1, 4, 6, 8, 13, 20. We realize that this is a time when "Yahweh takes action," one way of translating a similar reference in Ps. 118:24 (cf. Gösta W. Ahlström, *Joel and the Temple Cult of Jerusalem,* 66, n. 1), or according to a more precise translation of the opening salvo in Zech. 14:1, "Look! A day has come for Yahweh."

Typical of apocalyptic style, Yahweh responds to the nations who invaded Jerusalem and cruelly abused its inhabitants (vv. 1-2) by proclaiming a "holy war" against them (vv. 12-15). In between a marvelous description is given of the Lord's transformation of Jerusalem and the Holy Land (vv. 3-11). The various movements throughout this chapter all center vigorously around Jerusalem, with intense activity directed toward or away from the Holy City and culminating in the pilgrimage of even some gentile people for the messianic Feast of Tabernacles or Booths (vv. 16-21).

This important feast with an octave of celebrations enabled Israel not only to hear reaffirmed the initial promises of the land but also to enjoy its full abundance symbolically in ceremonial feasting and rejoicing. Especially as enunciated in the book of Deuteronomy, liturgy blended the earlier day of promise and the final day of fulfillment. Deuteronomy resonates with the word "today" and with the first person "we" or "us." In answer to a child's question, "What is the meaning of these ceremonies?" the parents answer:

> We were Pharaoh's slaves in Egypt; and the Lord brought us out of Egypt with a mighty hand; and the Lord showed signs and wonders, great and grievous . . . before *our* eyes . . . that he might bring us in and give us the land. (Deut. 6:21-23)

And as Deut 5:3 adds:

> Not with our ancestors did the LORD make this covenant, but *with us, all of us who are alive here this day.* (author's translation)

In a study of the prophecy of *Joel and the Temple Cult of Jerusalem,* Ahlström indicates that liturgy can so enhance the action of God in what is being commemorated and reenacted, and so accentuate God's presence in the midst of worship, that liturgy takes on many of the qualities normally associated with apocalyptic style. Because one of the most important feasts of Judaism is being featured, this passage of Zechariah may be more liturgical in character and less purely apocalyptic or eschatological than is generally thought.

APOCALYPTIC BUT NOT FINAL

Many trademarks normally associated with apocalyptic style show up. Some of these are rather new; others are common to other biblical patterns of writing or speaking, only more conspicuously present. For instance:

(1) *Older traditions and motifs* are woven into the text, like the story of the plagues in Egypt (Zech. 14:12; Exod. 7–11), water flowing from the temple (Zech. 14:8; Ps. 46:4; Ezek. 47:1-12; Joel 3:18), the Feast of Booths or Tabernacles (Zech. 14:16-19; see references below), the nations' attack against Jerusalem (v. 2; Isa. 10:5-6; Jer. 6:4-8).

(2) *Surrealistic symbols* break geological or geographical laws, such as the collapse or splitting of mountains (Zech. 14:4; Ps. 46:2; 114:3-4), streams of water flowing east and west from Jerusalem, differently than what the normal watershed of the country permits

(Zech. 14:8; Gen. 2:10), continuous daylight (Zech. 14:7; Isa. 60:19-20).

(3) *Cataclysmic struggles* are fought between forces of evil and goodness (Zech. 14:2-3; Ezek. 38–39), with an abundant use of words and images from the "holy" or "*herem*-extermination" war (dividing of spoils, capture and plunder, smiting and cutting off, panic and fear; Exod. 15:1-18; Judg. 5), with dreadful consequences such as the rotting of eyes in their sockets (Zech. 14:12; Ezek. 38:21-22; 39:18-20).

(4) *God alone* wages this war as a mighty warrior standing atop the Mount of Olives (Zech. 14:4; Isa. 24:21-23; 25:10-12).

This type of warfare is entirely beyond the resources of postexilic Israel, so that the description must be symbolic of God's complete victory over cosmic forces of evil. Literature such as this, symbolic though it be, is declaring the very real fact that individually and corporately we are engaged in a moral battle that will swallow us in defeat unless we turn with faith to God.

As seen frequently enough in Zechariah, important words and ideas stitch each new chapter into the pattern of previous chapters. With Zech. 12:1–13:9, ch. 14 speaks of the nations' attack against Jerusalem. In accord with the first vision (1:7-17), the text exhibits anger toward the nations and compassion exclusively for Jerusalem, yet without complete consistency. A remnant of the nations is invited to participate in the liturgy of the Feast of Booths (14:16) and to dwell in Jerusalem (2:10-12). As noted already, other key ideas in ch. 14 are found to occur especially in the preceding section of the prophecy. The editor of the entire book certainly viewed the final chapter as a climax subsuming everything within God's battle for Jerusalem and within the celebration of the Feast of Booths.

It is not certain whether the editor intended to write about the *absolutely final* day of the Lord, in truly eschatological style, as we find it described, for instance, in Isa. 65–66, when "no more shall be heard in it the sound of weeping and the cry of distress," and "they shall not labor in vain, or bear children for calamity" (Isa. 65:19, 23). In Zech. 14:18-19 God is still actively punishing the enemy, and when v. 16 speaks about "everyone that *survives* of all the nations," an aspect of weakness appears in our picture of the celebration of Booths. It is worth noting, moreover, that the dimensions of the promised land in v. 10 ("from Geba to Rimmon south of Jerusalem") do not reach even the narrower limits of the country "from Dan to Beer-sheba" (Judg. 20:1; 1 Sam. 3:20; 2 Sam. 3:10), much less the wider sweep into Transjordan and Lebanon foreseen earlier in Zech. 10:10. Geba is only 6 miles north of Jerusalem, Rimmon only 35 miles southwest of Jerusalem, not the 45 miles to Beersheba. The final verse, "that there shall no longer be a trader in the house of the LORD of hosts on that day," seems almost as much a warning against traders as it is a declaration about their absence. In any case, 14:21 is anticlimactic for a final, eschatological view of Israel. For these reasons it may not be entirely correct to speak of ch. 14 as fully eschatological.

MESSIANIC FEAST OF BOOTHS

In speaking of the messianic aspect of the Feast of Booths, we are referring to messianism without a messiah! *Messiah* is almost a formal transliteration of a Hebrew word meaning *the anointed one.* It applied first to the king (1 Sam. 10:1; 16:13) and then by extension to the high priest (Lev. 8:12). Eventually the Dead Sea Scrolls will refer to the two Messiahs, one of Aaron (the priestly Messiah) and the other of Israel (the royal, Davidic Messiah)—cf. 1QS 9:11.

We have observed the transition in Zechariah whereby the person of Zerubbabel and therefore the figure of the royal messiah have been merged with that of the high priest and so have disappeared (Zech. 3:1-10; 6:9-14), with only a brief surfacing in 9:9-10. At the end of Zechariah's prophecy God alone is king (14:16) and temple liturgy is central. There is little or no need for a Davidic king, especially in the shrunken size of the country. Royal Davidic messianism remains as a distant hope when God, not military might, will revive the dynasty; such was the interpretation given in the late postexilic age to such passages as Ps. 2:7; 110:3; Isa. 11:1-2; Matt. 22:41-46. Messianic understanding tended to eliminate the messiah of the royal Davidic line and to speak only of God or of the priesthood.

It frequently happens in the Bible (and also today) that smallness enables a people to dream greatness and to celebrate those dreams symbolically in the liturgy. Such hopes, a more theological word for dreams, are built out of the memory of God's great, redemptive acts of the past that become the pledge of God's continuing action into the future. As Gabriel Marcel wrote paradoxically: "hope is the memory of the future." Liturgy fleshes out such a memory in words and ceremonies congruent with the contemporary moment, yet in so intense a way as to be promising us the future, indeed of already anticipating that future. Theologians at times call this phenomenon "realized eschatology." If we observe the various stages of development in the Feast of Booths, we see how memory led Israel forward into a glorious future. The Feast of Booths was one of the oldest pilgrimage festivals, alluded to already in Judg. 21:19 and 1 Sam. 1:3, and it continued to occupy such importance that in a number of places it was simply called "the feast" (Ps. 81:3; 1 Kgs. 8:2; Ezek. 45:25; Neh. 8:14). See George W. MacRae, "The Meaning and Evolution of the Feast of Tabernacles," *CBQ* 22 (1960): 251-276, especially 268-270; Walter Harrelson, "The Celebration of the Feast of Booths according to Zech 14,16-21," *Religions in Antiquity,* 88-96.

According to the major biblical descriptions of this feast we can trace its development from the past into the future:

Leviticus 23:33-44 stresses God's protection of the Israelites during their desert wandering when they dwelt in booths or tents.

Deuteronomy 16:13-15 focuses instead upon the land of Canaan and the merry-making at the final harvest festival of grapes and olives, in our month of October. Because this time marked the end of the dry season, it was but natural to pray for rain, especially the early and late rains before and after the normal winter rains (see Zech. 10:1). An abundant rainfall insured fertile crops, good harvest, and full cisterns for the year ahead.

1 Kings 8 reveals another important shift in the meaning of the feast. Solomon dedicates the temple on the Feast of Tabernacles. He achieved a radical transition in practice and theology, something not permitted to David (2 Sam. 7:1-7). Up till now the ark of the covenant never had a permanent dwelling place, especially if we understand the temple at Shiloh (1 Sam. 1–4) to be a tent like that in the desert with Moses and Aaron. The feast gratefully acknowledged Yahweh's protection or "tabernacling" of the people from the heat in the wilderness and from hunger in the land. Solomon now undertook to "protect" Yahweh in the tabernacle that he would build. While previously the ark moved with the people, to provide strength in times of danger (Num. 10:35; Pss. 68 and 132; 1 Sam. 4:2-5), now the ark remains ever more permanently in the temple, generally secluded from the eyes of everyone but the high priest, and people come on pilgrimage to the place of the ark.

The glorious temple of King Solomon enabled the feast to be a time for rallying in God's presence. All Israel journeyed to Jerusalem, and Zechariah anticipates foreigners to come as well. According to Deut. 11, people looked to Yahweh for the all-important gift of rain. Their prayer was reenacted as though symbolically fulfilled, by bringing water from the pool of Siloam, pouring it into a silver bowl near the altar, and performing libations through the eight days of the octave of the feast (see *The Mishnah,* trans. Herbert Danby [New York and Oxford: Oxford University Press, 1933], 1790). So important were these prayers and ceremony that according to Zechariah rain would be withheld from "any of the families of the earth [who] do not go up to Jerusalem to worship the King, the LORD of hosts" (Zech. 14:17). Moreover, "if any family of Egypt does not go up and present themselves, then upon them shall not come the plague" (v. 18 author's translation). The word "not" is added to the translation of the RSV from the Hebrew text, meaning that some other punishment will be inflicted upon Egypt, a land that normally does not depend upon rain but upon flooding and irrigation from the river Nile. The featuring of candles and lights in the celebration of Tabernacles may have induced the earlier reference to "continuous day[light]" in v. 7. The ceremony with water may have led to the reference to an inexhaustible flow of water from the temple in v. 8.

The pouring of water at the Feast of Booths became a pivotal moment for remembering other biblical references. Some of these have already been mentioned, especially regarding the stream of water that flowed from the altar. This brought to mind the rock struck by Moses in the wilderness (Exod. 17:6; Num. 20:11). This rock came to be described ever more exotically, as in Ps. 78:15-16, where rivers flowed from it, or in Ps. 81:16, where it flowed "with honey [to] satisfy you," or again in Sir. 24:23-29, where it is associated with the teaching of the law at the temple and so became the source of the four rivers of paradise (Gen. 2:10-14). This was the rock that later tradition declared to follow the Israelites through the desert and was subsumed in the life-giving person of Christ: "They drank from the supernatural Rock which followed them, and the Rock was Christ" (1 Cor. 10:4).

As each festival of Tabernacles was celebrated, the present moment anticipated the future as it lived from the past. Liturgy kept the past fully alive by imparting a symbolic meaning to it. This symbolism presumes the reality of the past to be so vibrant and so real that it permeated the entire environment of the present moment and was enfleshed in its details. Because God was the principal actor of the past and the center of devotion in the present as well as the provider of the future fulfillment, liturgy accomplished its blending of past, present, and future by centering all attention upon the presence of God in the moment of worship.

This eschatological background to the Feast of Tabernacles explains an incident at the transfiguration of Jesus. The apostles, seeing

Jesus in dazzling glory on the mountain speaking with Moses and Elijah, declare: "Master, it is well that we are here; *let us make three booths,* one for you and one for Moses and one for Elijah" (Luke 9:33). They felt that the heavenly Feast of Booths had begun!

ENHANCEMENT OF THE SECULAR OR OF THE SACRED

Some writers detect in the final verses of Zech. 14 "shocking words for an OT priest . . . when every distinction between the holy and the profane will be eliminated" (cf. Ralph L. Smith, *Micah—Malachi,* 293). Zechariah states that "every pot in Jerusalem and Judah shall be sacred," and even "the bells of the horses [shall be inscribed with words from the turban of the high priest], 'Holy to the LORD'" (cf. 3:9). Yet the temple and its ceremonies are the source of holiness, especially at the Feast of Booths.

The temple extends its sacred character outward to embrace the entire life of the devout Israelite. Just as the early "secular" life of the Israelite people, as they fled from Egypt or dwelt in tents in the wilderness, supplied the images for the sacred ceremonies of Passover and Booths, now the ceremonies are communicating their sacredness to the homes and activities of the people. In order for people to recognize the presence of God in their homes, they need the strong reminder of God's presence in the temple. For them to see the protective presence of God in their daily life, they are greatly assisted by the temple ritual in which the sacred stories about Moses, Joshua, and other people of faith are acted out anew through processions, sacred meals, and other liturgical actions. Each new generation thus participated in the Exodus and in the miraculous feeding in the wilderness.

The Feast of Booths associated the temple with the homes of the people. Each family built their own *sukkah* or booth, as described in Neh. 8:15-18, and here they lived for the eight days of the feast. It was the temple that imparted its holiness to the home, just as the life that flowed from the temple altar was manifested by the "branches of olive, wild olive, myrtle, palm, and other leafy trees" that adorned the individual *sukkoth* or booths of the people (Neh. 8:15). These types of trees have a religious character about them. The night rider whom Zechariah saw in the first vision was "standing among the myrtle trees in the glen." The trees that will be miraculously planted in the wasteland, according to a song of Second Isaiah, consist of "the cedar, the acacia, the myrtle, and the olive, . . . the cypress, the plane and the pine together" (Isa. 41:19). The details of the Feast of Booths, therefore, carry a heavy overtone of sacred symbolism. Without the temple and its liturgy this sacredness could be easily swallowed up by secular concerns.

Just as the life of the inhabitants of Jerusalem was being more and more absorbed within a theocracy with the high priest in charge, likewise the sacredness of the temple was extending its holiness throughout the city and into every detail of people's lives. In some way this was Zechariah's final answer to the prophecy of Haggai that "the latter splendor of this house shall be greater than the former, . . . and in this place I will give prosperity [Hebrew *shalom*], says the LORD of hosts" (Hag. 2:9). Because Haggai's exhortation had been obeyed and the temple rebuilt, the temple in its turn has now assured the people that their entire city was as sacred and as enduring as the house of God.

While Haggai accomplished the rebuilding of the temple, Zechariah through his visions enhanced the role of the high priest and saw to the removal of all uncleanness from the temple and from the city. Then in the second part of the prophecy (Zech. 9–14) Zechariah made Jerusalem ever more emphatically the center of world history and the heart or navel of living for every Israelite man or woman (cf. Ezek. 38:12). Even some of the foreigners will join the Israelites in pilgrimage to Jerusalem.

In this context the final verse of Zechariah takes on new meaning: "there shall no longer be a trader [in Hebrew the word is spelled the same as 'Canaanite'; see 11:7, 11] in the house of the LORD of hosts on that day." Zechariah is extending the canopy of the sacred over foreigners. There is this proviso: everyone must worship Yahweh and join in Israel's traditions of the Exodus out of Egypt and the settlement of the land of Canaan, at least symbolically, by celebrating the Feast of Booths. The Jerusalem temple is beginning to reach out and consecrate the rest of the world.

BIBLIOGRAPHY

Books

Ackroyd, Peter R. *Exile and Restoration: A Study of Hebrew Thought of the Sixth Century B.C.* Old Testament Library (Philadelphia: Westminster and London: SCM, 1968).

Ahlström, Gösta W. *Joel and the Temple Cult of Jerusalem*. Supplements to Vetus Testamentum 21 (Leiden: Brill, 1971).

Amsler, Samuel, Lacocque, André, and Vuilleumier, René. *Aggée, Zacharie 1–8, Zacharie 9–14, Malachie*. Commentaire de l'Ancien Testament 11c (Neuchatel: Delachaux & Niestlé, 1981).

Baldwin, Joyce G. *Haggai, Zechariah, Malachi*. Tyndale Old Testament Commentaries (Downers Grove and Leicester: Inter-Varsity Press, 1972).

Blenkinsopp, Joseph. *A History of Prophecy in Israel* (Philadelphia: Westminster, 1983 and London: SPCK, 1984).

Bruce, Frederick Fyvie. *New Testament Development of Old Testament Themes* (Grand Rapids: Wm. B. Eerdmans and Exeter: Paternoster, 1968).

Carroll, Robert P. *When Prophecy Failed: Cognitive Dissonance in the Prophetic Traditions of the Old Testament* (New York: Seabury, 1979).

Chary, Théophane. *Aggée–Zacharie Malachie*. Sources Bibliques (Paris: J. Gabalda, 1969).

———. *Les Prophètes et le culte à partir de l'exil* (Paris: Editions Desclée, 1955).

Childs, Brevard S. *Introduction to the Old Testament as Scripture* (Philadelphia: Fortress, 1979 and London: SCM, 1983).

Clements, Ronald E. *Isaiah and the Deliverance of Jerusalem*. Journal for the Study of the Old Testament, Supplement 13 (Sheffield: University of Sheffield, 1980).

Danby, Herbert, trans.. *The Midrash* (New York and Oxford: Oxford University Press, 1933).

Dhorme, Édouard P. *La Bible*. 2 vols. Bibliothèque de la Pléiade 139 (Paris: Editions Gallimard, 1956-1959).

Dodd, C. H. *According to the Scriptures* (New York: Scribners and London: James Nisbet, 1953).

Douglas, Mary. *Purity and Danger* (1966; repr. New York: Methuen, 1984).

Epstein, Isidore, ed. *The Babylonian Talmud,* 35 vols. (London: Soncino Press, 1935-1948).

Finegan, Jack. *Handbook of Biblical Chronology* (Princeton: Princeton University Press, 1964).

Hanson, Paul D. *The Dawn of Apocalyptic,* 2nd ed. (Philadelphia: Fortress, 1979).

Huber, Friedrich. *Jahwe, Juda und die anderen Völker beim Propheten Jesaja* (New York and Berlin: Walter de Gruyter, 1976).

Jones, Douglas R. *Haggai, Zechariah and Malachi.* Torch Bible Commentaries (London: SCM, 1962).

Keel, Othmar. *The Symbolism of the Biblical World* (New York: Seabury, 1978).

Knight, George A. F. *The New Israel: Isaiah 56–66.* International Theological Commentary (Grand Rapids: Wm. B. Eerdmans and Edinburgh: Handsel, 1985).

Kodell, Jerome, *Lamentations, Haggai, Zechariah, Malachi, Obadiah, Joel, Second Zechariah, Baruch.* Old Testament Message 14 (Wilmington, DE: Michael Glazier, 1982).

Lacocque, André. *Zacharie 9–14. See* Amsler, Samuel.

Lamarche, Paul. *Zacharie IX–XIV: Structure littéraire et messianisme.* Études Bibliques (Paris: J. Gabalda, 1961).

Martin-Achard, Robert, and Re'emi, S. Paul. *God's People in Crisis: Amos and Lamentations.* International Theological Commentary (Grand Rapids: Wm. B. Eerdmans and Edinburgh: Handsel, 1984).

Mason, Rex. *The Books of Haggai, Zechariah, and Malachi.* The Cambridge Bible Commentary on the New English Bible (New York and Cambridge: Cambridge University Press, 1977).

Mitchell, H. G. T., Smith, J. M. P., and Brewer, Julius A. *Haggai, Zechariah, Malachi and Jonah.* International Critical Commentary (New York: Scribner and Edinburgh: T. & T. Clark, 1912).

Odelain, Olivier, and Seguineau, Raymond. *Dictionary of Proper Names and Places in the Bible* (Garden City, NJ: Doubleday, 1981).

Otzen, Benedikt. *Studien über Deuterosacharja.* Acta Theologica Danica 6 (Copenhagen: Prostant apud Munksgaard, 1964).

Petersen, David L. *Haggai and Zechariah 1–8.* Old Testament Library (Philadelphia: Westminster and London: SCM, 1984).

——. *Late Israelite Prophecy: Studies in Deutero-Prophetic Literature and in Chronicles.* Society of Biblical Literature Monograph 23 (Missoula, MT: Scholars Press, 1977).

Petitjean, Albert. *Les Oracles du Proto-Zacharie: Un programme de restauration pour la communauté juive après l'exil.* Études Bibliques (Paris: J. Gabalda and Louvain: Éditions Impr. orientaliste, 1969).

Re'emi, S. Paul. *See* Martin-Achard.

Saebo, Magne. *Sacharja 9–14: Untersuchungen von Text und Form.* Wissenschaftliche Monographien zum Alten und Neuen Testament 34 (Neukirchen-Vluyn: Neukirchener Verlag, 1969).

163

Sellin, Ernst. *Studien zur Entstehungsgeschichte der judischen Gemeinde nach dem babylonischen Exil,* 2 vols. (Leipzig: A. Deichert, 1900-1901).

Smith, George Adam. *The Book of the Twelve Prophets,* 2 vols. Expositor's Bible. (New York: George H. Doran and London: Hodder & Stoughton, 1898).

Smith, Ralph L. *Micah–Malachi.* Word Biblical Commentary 32 (Waco, TX: Word Books, 1984).

Stronach, David. *Pasargadae* (New York and Oxford: Oxford University Press, 1978).

Stuhlmueller, Carroll. *Psalms,* 2 vols. Old Testament Message 21-22 (Wilmington, DE: Michael Glazier, 1983).

Vawter, Bruce. *The Conscience of Israel: Pre-exilic Prophets and Prophecy.* (New York: Sheed and Ward, 1961).

Willi-Plein, Ina. *Prophetie am Ende: Untersuchungen zu Sacharja 9–14.* Bonner Biblische Beiträge 42 (Cologne: Peter Hanstein, 1974).

Würthwein, Ernst. *The Text of the Old Testament* (Grand Rapids: Wm. B. Eerdmans and London: SCM, 1979).

Articles

Ackroyd, Peter R. "Haggai," in *Peake's Commentary on the Bible,* ed. Matthew Black (New York: Thomas Nelson, 1962), 643-645.

———. "Zechariah," in *Peake's Commentary on the Bible,* 646-655.

Barth, Christoph. "gyl," *Theological Dictionary of the Old Testament* 2, ed. G. Johannes Botterweck and Helmer Ringgren, rev. ed. (Grand Rapids: Wm. B. Eerdmans: 1977), 470-75.

Carroll, Robert P. "Twilight of Prophecy or Dawn of Apocalyptic?" *Journal for the Study of the Old Testament* 14 (1979): 3-35.

Delcor, Matthias. "Un problème de critique textuelle et d'exégèse: Zach., XII, 10," *Revue Biblique* 58 (1951): 189-199.

———. "Les sources du Deutéro-Zacharie et ses procédés d'emprunt," *Revue Biblique* 59 (1952): 385-411.

Dentan, Robert C. "The Book of Zechariah, Chapters 9–14: Introduction and Exegesis," *The Interpreter's Bible,* ed. George A. Buttrick, 6 (Nashville: Abingdon, 1956) 1089-1114.

Guillet, Jacques. "God," *Dictionary of Biblical Theology,* ed. Xavier Léon-Dufour, 2nd ed. (New York: Seabury, 1973), 205-212.

Halpern, Baruch. "The Ritual Background of Zechariah's Temple Song," *Catholic Biblical Quarterly* 40 (1978): 167-190.

Harrelson, Walter. "The Celebration of the Feast of Booths according to Zech 14,16-21," *Religions in Antiquity.* Festschrift E. R. Goodenough, ed. Jacob Neusner. *Studies in the History of Religion.* Supplements to Numen 14 (Leiden: Brill, 1968): 88-96.

Lipiński, Edward. "Recherches sur le livre de Zacharie," *Vetus Testamentum* 20 (1970): 25-55.

MacRae, George W. "The Meaning and Evolution of the Feast of Tabernacles," *Catholic Biblical Quarterly* 22 (1960): 251-276.

Mason, Rex A. "The Purpose of the 'Editorial Framework' of the Book of Haggai," *Vetus Testamentum* 27 (1977): 413-421.

———. "The Relation of Zech 9–14 to Proto-Zechariah," *Zeitschrift für die alttestamentliche Wissenschaft* 88 (1976): 227-239.

———. "Some Echoes of the Preaching in the Second Temple? Tradition Elements in Zechariah 1–8," *Zeitschrift für die alttestamentliche Wissenschaft* 96 (1984): 221-235.

Mauch, Theodor M. "Zechariah," *The Interpreter's Dictionary of the Bible*, ed. George A. Buttrick, 4 (Nashville: Abingdon, 1962): 941-43.

Neuenzeit, Paul. "Time," *Encyclopedia of Biblical Theology*, ed. J. B. Bauer (New York: Crossroad, 1981), 911-15.

Petersen, David L. "Zechariah's Visions: A Theological Perspective," *Vetus Testamentum* 34 (1984): 195-206.

———. "Zerubbabel and Jerusalem Temple Reconstruction," *Catholic Biblical Quarterly* 36 (1974): 366-372.

Speers, Theodore C. "The Book of Zechariah, Chapters 1–8: Exposition," *The Interpreter's Bible* 6 (1956): 1056-1114.

Stuhlmueller, Carroll. "Haggai, Zechariah, Malachi," *Jerome Biblical Commentary*, ed. Raymond E. Brown, Joseph A. Fitzmyer, and Roland E. Murphy (Englewood Cliffs: Prentice-Hall, 1968), 387-401.

———. "Post-Exilic Period: Spirit, Apocalyptic," *Jerome Biblical Commentary*, 337-343.

Torrey, Charles C. "The Foundry of the Second Temple at Jerusalem," *Journal of Biblical Literature* 55 (1936): 247-260.

Watts, J. D. W. "Zechariah," *The Broadman Bible Commentary* 7 (Nashville: Broadman, 1972): 308-365.

Widengren, Geo. "The Persian Period," in *Israelite and Judaean History*, ed. John H. Hayes and J. Maxwell Miller. Old Testament Library (Philadelphia: Westminster and London: SCM, 1977), 489-538.